Sales Talk in Japan and the United States

*An ethnographic analysis
of contrastive speech events*

Aoi Tsuda, S.N.D.

Georgetown University Press, Washington, D.C. 20057

Copyright © 1984 by Georgetown University Press
Printed in the United States of America
Library of Congress Cataloging in Publication Data
Tsuda, Aoi.
   Sales talk in Japan and the United States.

   Bibliography: p.
   1. Sociolinguistics. 2. Speech acts (Linguistics) 3. Sales—Japan—
Language. 4. Sales—United States—Language. I. Title.

P40.T8   1984   401'.9   84-1568
ISBN -087840-213-6

To the Hill family,

who by their loving acceptance of me into
their home and their hearts showed me a
beautiful living example of the Christian
faith which reaches beyond space and cultural differences.

CONTENTS

ACKNOWLEDGMENTS

This book would not have been possible without the cooperation and support of countless people. I am deeply grateful to all of them for their invaluable inspiration and stimulation. I must especially mention the following: Dr. Felix Lobo, S.J., Professor at Sophia University, Tokyo, and Director of the Sophia Linguistic Institute for International Communication, who opened up to me the unfathomable world of linguistics and urged me to pursue my interest in this field; Dr. Muriel Saville-Troike of the University of Illinois, who was a professor of Linguistics at Georgetown University at the time of my doctoral studies there and who made helpful comments on a preliminary version of this work; and Dr. Ralph Fasold and Dr. Roger Shuy, Professors of Linguistics at Georgetown, who shared with me their deep insights into sociolinguistics.

I owe much also to all the salespeople, customers, and many others both in Japan and the United States who made my research possible. And my special gratitude is extended to the Sisters of Notre Dame de Namur at Trinity College, Washington, D.C,, for their loving, warm hospitality and constant encouragement during my four and a half years' stay in a foreign land.

Finally, I am deeply indebted to the several organizations which relieved me of financial worries and made it possible for me to devote these years entirely to attainment of my goal. Chief among these are the Fulbright grant, the American Association of University Women (AAUW), and the Philanthropic Educational Organization (PEO).

CHAPTER ONE

INTRODUCTION

1.1 Culture and mode of communication. Anthropology has clarified that the culture of a given society is the beliefs, shared ideals, values, and standards of behavior which are transmitted in a manner acceptable to the members of succeeding generations of that society. Since they share a common culture, members of the same society can predict each others' actions in specific circumstances and react accordingly. Therefore when we meet people from different cultures and see them behave differently from us, we may think that their behavior is somewhat strange, awkward, impolite, or even rude.

As a member of an international religious congregation, I have lived more than ten years in international communities both in Japan and the United States. Even now, after these years of experience, my continued reflections lead to a deeper awareness and new insights into the differences of the value systems of the two cultures. My first contact with the 'foreigners' began about 20 years ago, when I entered a Catholic high school in Japan. My encounter with American missionaries at that time brought a very exciting and totally new experience. They not only spoke 'beautiful' English, a language which I was eager to master, but also were dressed in a dignified religious habit which injected an exotic note in the land of Buddhism. They were full of spirit and sometimes their vitality, so happily and actively expressed even in a different cultural setting, caused the young high school student to wonder and admire. However, I was much disappointed with one of the missionaries when I saw her blow her nose noisily, holding her handkerchief in only one hand, in front of all the students. My reaction was simply due to the fact that Japanese children are always trained to blow their nose quietly with both hands, and in the absence of other people, if possible. Therefore, I thought that the missionary teacher who had a bad cold was rather rude and did not know how to conduct herself in the classroom. That episode was a great shock to me, because I evaluated my teacher's behavior according to the standards and value system of my own Japanese culture.

1

Now, almost 20 years later, I find myself in the United States, doing the same thing with a grim smile that the American missionary did without any hesitation. I am learning a second culture.

My second reflection regarding cultural differences deals with a Japanese girl who enrolled in college in the United States to study American history. She returned to Japan to spend a summer with her parents but when she came back to the United States again, she looked sad and told one of her American teachers: 'I think I should admit that my parents do not love me any more.' The teacher asked why, and the girl explained very seriously: 'When I saw my parents at the airport in Tokyo, they did not kiss me. They did not hug me. They did not even hurry to me to say, "welcome home." Instead, they bowed deeply and quietly several times, keeping some distance from me.' This episode indicates that once we are out of our own country and are comfortable and confident in a new culture, we are liable to forget the value system of our native culture. In the case of this student, the value of the traditional greeting behavior, showing respect and love between parents and children in Japan, was replaced by the different value system to which she had been exposed in a new culture.

Another interesting aspect of culture in relation to perception and interpretation of a certain event is shown in the following story. I was invited to an Italian dinner one night at the home of an Italian-American family. When I was served spaghetti it was so delicious that I accepted when the hostess offered a second helping. Since it was served in a big plate, I was almost full when I finished the second portion. However, I was surprised and embarrassed when I found out that the spaghetti was served only as an appetizer before the main course, which consisted of several dishes and was followed by assorted desserts. Spaghetti is served in Japan as well as at an Italian dinner, but not just as an appetizer. Thus, I had not actually participated in an authentic Italian dinner until I came to the United States. This small anecdote indicates that the value and role of a certain item is different in different cultures, even though we can find the same item in both cultures.

Each of the three examples I have cited manifests the mutual relationship between culture and patterns of communication. Each culture influences and sometimes conditions our behavior and the evaluation of our behavior. In addition, every language expresses how its speakers interpret reality in culture-specific ways. For example, suppose we examine a group of children (siblings, born of the same parents). English describes these siblings with two terms, *brother* and *sister*. Thus, the siblings are divided into two categories, brother and sister. In contrast, Japanese describes the siblings by means of four words: *ani* 'elder brother', *otōto* 'younger brother', *ane* 'elder sister', and *imōto* 'younger sister'. Thus, by including another feature, namely, age, in addition to sex, the group is divided into four categories, i.e., older brother, younger brother, older sister, younger sister. In the case of Turkish, the same reality is signified by three kin terms, since the criterion sex is applied only for the elder brother or elder sister. Again, this simple example shows how each language recognizes the same phenomenon differently, at least on a vocabulary level.

1.2 Culture and conversational style. When we pay careful attention to conversational style in our daily life, we notice that even a simple greeting formula in different cultures manifests a specific pattern. In other words, each culture teaches what is appropriate to express and the appropriate way to express it.

The following conversational exchanges may attract the attention of those who are interested in language use in a specific situation where each of the conversationalists belongs to a different language background. The conversations are some of the early morning greetings exchanged over a two-year period between an American scholar of Japanese, stationed in Japan and working in a Japanese company, and his landlady (Seward 1968).

Every morning at the entrance of the house, Mr. Seward was asked by his landlady *Odekake desu ka?* 'Are you going out?' as she saw him leave for work. For months he simply answered *Hai dekakemasu* 'Yes, I am going out', but little by little, he began to wonder if that expression of greeting might have a 'sinister design'. Therefore he tried the following responses.

Conversation 1:
Landlady: Odekake desu ka? 'Are you going out?'
Seward:　 Chigaima su. 'No, I'm not.'
Landlady: A sō desu ka? De wa itte irasshai.
　　　　　 'Oh, is that so? Well, good-bye.'

After this conversation, Seward left the house as usual. The next morning, he had the following conversation with the landlady.

Conversation 2:
Landlady: Odekake desu ka? 'Are you going out?'
Seward:　 Dekakemasen. 'I'm not going out.'
Landlady: De wa, itte irasshai. 'Well, good-bye.'

The morning after that, Seward and the landlady exchanged greetings as follows.

Conversation 3:
Landlady: Odekake desu ka? 'Are you going out?'
Seward:　 Kyō uchi ni orimasu. 'I will stay at home today.'
Landlady: Itte irasshai. 'Good-bye.'

Seward states (1968:46):

I tried a few more times after that but my heart was not in
it. Perhaps she did not really listen to what I said--or
perhaps she was making allowances, as may often have been
necessary--for the caprices of a barbaric American. Over
the years the patience of the Orient finally bested me... I
learned that you can't hustle--or change--the East.

Seward remarks that this was not the only problem he had in
greeting the landlady. He was also bothered by another expression which is frequently used as a greeting in Japanese: *Dochira e?* 'Where are you going?'

For years I was unable to fully suppress a feeling of irri-
tation when someone I hardly knew asked me where I was
going, and so, in defense, I devised and used a variety of
retorts hopefully designed to abash such interrogators.
Some I used are: *Yopparai ni mairimasu* 'I am going to
get juiced', *Sōri daijin to kinō no dekigoto wo sōdan
shite kuru* 'I'm going to discuss yesterday's events with
the prime minister', *Kanai no imōto to issho ni kisha-ōjō
wo toge ni ikimasu* 'My wife's younger sister and I are
going to throw ourselves in front of a train.' Although I
delivered these with stern face and a steely glance, I usually got no more than nervous titters in reply. Nor could I
detect any subsequent diminishing in the frequency of questions about my destination (Seward 1968:45).

Through the uncomfortable and frustrating experience of exchanging greetings with his landlady and his Japanese acquaintances, Seward finally understood what is implied in those
two greeting rituals in Japanese, and was able to give the following explanation (Seward 1968:46).

Nowadays when a man I scarcely know asks me *Dochira e?* I
smile a crooked smile and say *Chotto sokorahen made*
'Just down the street a ways'. He probably does not want to
know my destination, anyway.

These episodes remind us that the communication misfire between the Japanese landlady and the American 'hanger-on' was due
to the fact that they used different rules of speaking, even
though Japanese was their common channel of communication. In
the Japanese speech community, when in the greeting formula one
uses the equivalent of the English sentence *Where are you
going?*, the speaker neither intends to ask the destination nor
expects a definite response. The question is simply an equivalent of *Good morning,* or *Nice day,* or *You look very
nice today.* In other words, this specific sentence used in
greeting carries a special meaning which may be called the

cultural-social meaning, as opposed to literal meaning. However, the American interlocutor interpreted the utterance literally. He thought that the landlady was asking the exact place where he was going, and he could not understand why she was so curious and impolite. However, as the landlady had no intention of asking about his definite destination, she did not care how unusual his answers were, and she saw him off by saying *Itte irasshai* 'Good-bye.'

In other words, the landlady and the American scholar did not belong to the same speech community; Seward tried to communicate with the Japanese landlady in Japanese, but using English rules of speaking. There is no doubt that he could comprehend Japanese based on his linguistic competence in a narrow sense. His frustration was due to the fact that he did not have communicative competence in Japanese to deal with the ritual greeting formulas used in Japanese society. It is quite likely that he knew about Japanese as a formal system which relates an indefinite number of phonetic strings to semantic interpretation and had a good command of its grammatical structures. In order to communicate with the landlady, however, he not only had to understand the linguistic forms of the language but also had to know when, how and to whom it is appropriate to use his Japanese in a specific context, namely, in which context one such Japanese formula might be expressed.

1.3 The concept of speech community. Bloomfield (1933: 42) defines a speech community as a group of people who interact by means of speech. However, the exchanges described in section 1.2 indicate that in order to be considered a competent member of a certain speech community, one must also share knowledge of rules of speaking and interpretation of speech with other members of the community.

Through daily experiences as a teacher and as a student during the four years of my stay in the United States, I have become more and more aware of the truth of this statement. In the Japanese language class at Trinity College, Washington, D.C., which I was assigned to teach for two years, American students sometimes could not understand Japanese sentences because the situations in which the dialogues occurred were not familiar to them, and even more, they could not understand the way in which Japanese people think and express themselves in a specific context. Moreover, I myself occasionally make mistakes similar to those made by Seward in the examples cited. Here, even if the language being used is English, I sometimes recognize the fact that I speak English while using the rules of speaking of my native tongue, Japanese. My English is based on norms of interpretation in Japanese, not on those of American English. Hence, I occasionally find myself coming out with a question like the Japanese landlady's *Where are you going?* to one of my fellow teachers at Trinity College in Washington, even though I have no intention of asking a definite destination, but am merely trying to extend a simple greeting. I once noticed a friend's embarrassment in trying to maintain her privacy and at the same time to be polite to a friend from Japan when she said, *I have an off-campus appointment*. Clearly, the American friend interpreted the question on the basis of literal meaning, as everybody does in the American speech community in this context. These anecdotes point up the serious gap between what is usually expressed in grammar and what is actually communicated in a specific situation during the course of face-to-face interaction.

1.4   Sociolinguistics and ethnography of communication. Recent studies in sociolinguistics have shed light upon a number of issues important to the study of language in interaction with social life from a variety of linguistic, psychological, anthropological, and sociological perspectives. Hymes (1962, 1964a, 1964b, 1967a), Gumperz (1977), and Sherzer (1977), for example, point out that traditional grammatical analysis does not provide sufficient information on actual patterns of language usage. They emphasize that the totality of ways in which 'situated meaning' is expressed can be studied only on the basis of sociocultural assumptions concerning role and status relationship, social values, beliefs, and norms associated with various components in the actual speech event. Building on this principle, many ethnographers are now trying to formalize a general theory of interaction of language and social life encompassing the mutual relations between linguistic meaning and social significance. In other words, the research at which the ethnography of communication is aiming is the formulation of descriptive theories of speaking as a cultural system through investigation of the organization of speaking in social life. The relevant aspects of speaking as a cultural system include the system of community norms, principles, strategies, and values which characterize the speech activity as a whole in the community under consideration: 'In the first instance, description of speech events seeks to describe customary or culturally appropriate behavior' (Hymes 1972:62).

In order to attain this goal, ethnographers have an urgent need to collect data and supply information on cross-cultural speech events that are directly governed by rules or norms for the use of speech in different cultures. Gumperz (1977:192) states:

Ethnographers of speaking point out that there is a great lack of descriptive ethnographic information on the social norms of speaking, and therefore they have called for empirical cross-cultural research to fill this gap.

Similarly, Sherzer (1977:53) emphasizes the need for cross-cultural comparison in the framework of ethnography.

I began this critical assessment and appraisal of the ethnography of speaking by stressing the need for cross-cultural comparison and validity and I end it with a call for research in American society.

Motivated by these statements, I have already completed a pilot study of six speech events: (1) self-introduction, (2) greeting, (3) gift-giving, (4) leave-taking, (5) welcoming guests, and (6) introducing family members in the American and Japanese speech communities. Results of this pilot study indicate that each speech event in both speech communities is governed by culture-specific rules and norms for the use of speech. In the speech events just mentioned, my research demonstrates that each community has important and essential factors which make the speech event unique and distinct from the comparable one in the other speech community.

In regard to one example of a speech event from my pilot study, namely, that of self-introduction, I find that in the Japanese speech community a group identification is considered more important than personal status or names, especially when someone is going to identify himself/herself. The term 'group identification' means identification by the situational position of each individual rather than by the individuals' common features. In any society, individuals are gathered into social groups on the basis of an individual's circumstances and condition. The pilot study of the speech event of self-introduction indicates that Americans first identify themselves by their own names and their own jobs, which is uncommon or quite unusual in Japanese society. My data on this speech event between two Japanese female students indicates that, after knowing that they both came from Japan, the first means of identifying themselves was to share their background: to what educational institution they belong in Japan. It does not mean that they ignore each other's name, but that is a matter of secondary interest.

This observation and analysis correspond to the hypothesis of Japanese anthropologist Chie Nakane (Nakane 1970). Nakane finds two criteria illuminating and useful in describing Japanese society: 'attribute' and 'frame'. She uses 'attribute' to refer to being a member of a definite descent group that may be acquired not only by birth but also by achievement. By 'frame' she means a more circumstantial position of the individual. Thus, according to her analysis, 'taking industry as an example, "leather operator" or "executive" refers to "attribute" but "members of Y Company" refers to "frame"' (Nakane 1970:2).

In this way, to say that we belong to K University is a 'frame', but our own names are typical 'attributes' obtained by our own birth. Nakane explains that the two criteria 'attribute' and 'frame' usually overlap each other, but the primary concern is the relative degree of saliency in identification function between the two criteria. Her analysis, therefore, relates to the speech event of self-introduction between

Japanese people in this way: when a Japanese faces an outsider or nonacquaintance and affixes some position to himself/herself, he/she is inclined to give precedence to an institution as the 'frame' over an individual type of 'attribute'. Thus, taking the first speech event of self-introduction in my pilot study, it is clear that although American and Japanese speech communities have a similar speech event, this event encodes different beliefs, convictions, social values, and norms.

1.5 Topic for present investigation. I am presenting here observations on certain sales events in American and Japanese speech communities. One purpose of this research is to determine if the hypothesis presented by Nakane is true by conducting an analysis of two speech communities in regard to sales talk. The second purpose is to explicate the linguistic and cultural structure of sales talk in the Japanese speech community. It has not been my purpose at this time to make a structured statistical analysis of quantitative data. Although the analysis is extended to both the American and Japanese speech communities, the description and analysis of the American speech community are used primarily to investigate similarities and differences through the contrastive analysis of the two cultures, rather than to focus on the American events in their own right. After the overall pattern of the sales talk is described, emphasis is placed on concern for the ways in which cultural and social variation place constraints on or covary with linguistic variation in the Japanese speech community.

In order to approach this goal, the following procedures are necessary: (1) to describe and present a contrastive analysis of sales talk in American and Japanese speech communities; (2) to discover the nature of the communicative competence that enables members of each community to conduct and interpret speech; (3) to investigate social rules or norms that explain and constrain language behavior and behavior toward language in speech communities; (4) to determine how changes in the interaction of networks of speakers alter the ranges of their verbal repertoires; and finally, (5) to determine the symbolic value of language varieties for their speakers.

The approach which these procedures indicate naturally differs from the traditional approach to language which takes the linguistic form as a given code itself as the frame of reference abstracted from any context. The approach in this study, therefore, is to investigate communicative behaviors as a whole, taking as context a community, 'so that any given use of channel and code takes its place as but part of the resources upon which the members of the community draw' (Hymes 1964a). In this sense, this approach is concerned with language within a range of social contexts from a wider ethnographic and social perspective and pays serious attention to social and cultural factors as they relate to speech.

The study aims at responding to the urgent need for description and analysis of cross-cultural speech events first advocated by Hymes (1962).

1.6 Basic concept and framework. A salient characteristic of ethnographers of communication is their shared belief that the use of language cannot be effectively understood or analyzed outside the context of societal setting. Thus, according to the ethnographic point of view, a speech community is the starting point of analysis and the members of that community are the main source of shared knowledge through their communicative activities. Three basic units of communication are generally recognized for descriptive purposes: speech situation, speech event, and speech act. A speech situation is the context within which communication takes place, e.g. parties and meals. A speech event is a unit of communication relatively controlled by ways of speaking and norms for the use of speech, and usually involves the same participants focusing on a single topic. A speech act is coterminous with a single communicative function. On this basis, taking a meal with family members is a speech situation, a conversation during a meal is a speech event, and a joke within the conversation is a speech act. Therefore, many individual speech acts usually comprise a speech event and each speech event takes place within a speech situation. The same type of speech act can be observed in different speech events, e.g. a joke during a lecture in a classroom or during a homily in a liturgical setting. Similarly, the same type of speech event may occur in different speech situations, e.g. conversation during a birthday party or during an alumni meeting.

In order to describe the speech acts and speech events of a given community systematically and consistently, several components must be taken into consideration. Hymes (1972) suggests that the mnemonic *SPEAKING* represents these factors, although all are not always relevant, and the order in description may vary.

(1) Setting: refers to both physical and psychological environment as to the time and place as well as the cultural definition of the speech act or event.

(2) Participants: refers to speaker, hearer, occasionally to the audience witnessing the speech activity.

(3) Ends: refers to recognized and expected purpose of the speech act or event.

(4) Act sequence: refers to the actual sequences of speech acts exchanged between the participants during the specific speech event.

(5) Key: refers to the manner, tone, and spirit in which a speech act or event is performed, e.g. serious, painstaking.

(6) *Instrumentalities*: refers to channel of transmission of speech, e.g. oral, written, and the code which is used.

(7) *Norms*: refers both to norms of interpretation, or how speech acts within the event are to be understood, e.g. literally or metaphorically, and norms of interaction, or culturally based rules for appropriate communicative behaviors.

(8) *Genres*: refers to category of speech represented by the events, e.g. conversation, poem, letter.

The descriptive goal is to utilize these components, seeking both to see the relationship between various individual components and to recognize hierarchies of precedence among them in regard to actual usage within the speech community. Since any communicative behavior can be understood only in terms of the larger context of the society's total ethnography, a basic tenet is

the inseparability of sociolinguistic analysis from the full-scale analysis of social life; for it is in the analysis of social life that the requisite rules of selection for sociolinguistic features are to be found and stated (Hymes 1967a:27).

CHAPTER TWO

METHODOLOGY

2.1 Purpose of this investigation. This is an investigation, based on principles of ethnographic research, on sales talk in American and Japanese speech communities. More specifically, it is my aim (1) to analyze and present overall patterns of sales talk in American and Japanese communities, (2) to investigate social and cultural norms and values which govern the specific speech event in the speech communities under consideration, and (3) on the basis of these findings, to determine if Nakane's hypothesis discussed in Chapter 1 is valid with specific reference to salesmen's talk in the Japanese speech community.

After the general goal is accomplished, I focus on the ways of speaking in the Japanese speech community and examine the following points in detail: (1) how many different speech styles or varieties are being used by the participants, (2) what are the determining factors in selecting one code rather than another in different situations, and (3) what are the norms which govern the rules of speaking in different types of interactions between different types of salespeople and their customers.

2.2 General procedures. I returned to Japan on July 11, 1979 and engaged in field work there for six weeks. During my stay, I carried out the following projects: (1) collecting data pertaining to salesmen's talk; (2) conducting interviews with salespeople, and those who are preparing salespeople for their interactional experiences; (3) distributing questionnaires to salespeople and customers, and collecting the completed questionnaires. In addition to these main projects, I tried to acquire additional relevant information by means of: (1) obtaining handbooks, instructional literature for salespeople, and company pamphlets containing information for recognizing and interpreting speech patterns; (2) observing media presentations such as television and radio commercials which provided further insight into prevailing speech patterns; (3) reading and selecting samples of newspaper and magazine advertisements and

11

billboards providing additional material on the psychology of sales mannerisms typical of the speech community; and (4) reviewing books and articles in which salespeople discuss the secret of success in their fields.

After coming back to the United States late in August, 1979, I tried to repeat the process I had performed in Japan. Field work was begun on September 4, 1979 and was continued until April 4, 1980. After the research process was completed within the American speech community, I proceeded to the next task, listening to the tapes from both speech communities and selecting the data which I was to employ for the specific purpose of this analysis. The task of transcribing Japanese was begun in January, 1980 and completed by the end of February, 1980. Then some of the data were translated into English for the purpose of this research.

During the summer of 1980, I audited a business course on salesmanship at Georgetown University in order to benefit from the series of lectures about the principles of salesmanship and from the opportunity to participate in classroom discussion sessions on how to deal effectively with sales transactions. The course was very useful since it provided an excellent opportunity to learn about the psychology of selling and buying from experts in this field in the United States. Belonging as I do to the Japanese speech community, I believe that this experience was especially valuable since it gave me greater familiarity with sales transactions within that one of the two target speech communities of which I am not a member.

2.3 Method of collecting data in Japan. Salesmen can be classified in numerous categories with regard to the kinds of commodities and services they sell. In order to achieve consistency in this area of my research, I thought it would be realistic to limit the number of categories from which I would collect data. For this reason, before leaving for Japan, I decided tentatively to focus on sales transactions dealing with medicine, cosmetics, insurance, and cars. These specific categories were chosen because they were readily accessible and pertinent data could be gathered with comparative ease in a limited time. However, after six weeks of field work, the data collected ranged from the original four categories to additional types of sales dealing with vegetables, candies, fish, flowers, clothes, etc.

Salesmen can also be classified in regard to the following types: (1) institutional sales, (2) door-to-door sales, (3) department store sales, (4) sales in private stores, (5) sales on the street, (6) sales in markets, and (7) sales on trains.

Data were collected by three methods. (1) I visited various places where I thought sales transactions would likely take place (e.g. hospitals, shopping centers, markets, private stores, department stores, etc.). (2) Since sales transactions on public transportation vehicles are also popular in Japan, incidents of selling and buying on 'Shinkan-Sen', the Japanese bullet train between Tokyo and Nagoya, were used for gathering relevant data. (3) I visited the Japanese Sales Training Center in Tokyo and received permission from the president of that company to duplicate 17 taped examples of door-to-door salespeople's talk. Each of these contains an actual conversation between a salesperson and a customer. Among these 17 examples, the merchandise being dealt with varies, e.g. cars, insurance, books, sewing machines, etc. Since the purpose of the sales training center is to instruct door-to-door salespeople in effective merchandising techniques, there was a collection of taped data in which actual speeches were recorded for the purpose of reviews and discussions between sales trainers and salespeople. The president of the training center explained to me that each example was recorded by a sales trainer who accompanied a salesperson during an actual sales transaction.

2.3.1 Equipment and recording background. Except for the 17 examples of door-to-door sales talk obtained from Japan Sales Training Center, I undertook all the field work myself. Each tape was recorded by Sony Cassette-Corder TC-1100B. Since this model is small and features a built-in microphone, the participants involved in sales transactions were less suspicious throughout the recording period. As a matter of fact, at the shopping centers, markets, private stores, and department stores, no one except one saleslady in a department store inquired what I was doing or looked at me with curiosity or suspicion. The people, including salespeople, customers, and sometimes audiences, seemed to be busy and intent on their own activity. I pretended to be a prospective customer. Standing near the place where the sales transaction occurred, I recorded the actual speech. Therefore, I believe that spontaneous speech was recorded in natural situations.

For the data collected in the hospital, however, a totally different method was employed. First of all, through my brother, who is a heart surgeon living in Nagoya City, I was introduced to a specialist in internal medicine who is head of the department of internal medicine at a private hospital in Tokyo. This hospital was chosen because of its convenient location and the doctor's interested attitude.

After I explained the purpose of the research, the doctor promised to cooperate with the project. Sales transactions between drug companies and individual physicians in Japan are in the hands of a special type of salesperson known as 'proper'. The usual mode for such a salesperson in approaching a prospective client is to enter the physician's waiting room, identify himself as a sales representative to the receptionist, and wait until the doctor has finished seeing all his patients. When I was doing my research, four or five drug salespeople were usually on the waiting list daily for an interview with the doctor. After the doctor finished seeing his last patient, one of the nurses notified me as I waited outside his office and the doctor

let me sit beside him. As the door opened to admit each of
them, most of the salespersons showed some reaction at finding a
stranger seated beside the doctor. Some of them asked hesitant-
ly:

(1) Well, *Sensei*, is it all right to come in?
(2) Do you mind seeing me now?
(3) Am I interrupting you, *Sensei*?

The doctor replied:
(1) She is one of my relatives so she came to see me here.
(2) Please, she is my friend, so don't worry.
(3) Oh yes, please come in.

I would smile at the salesperson and greet him, *Good afternoon*. Generally, the salesperson was still hesitant but
responded *Oh, yes?* and began his speech. During the salesperson's talk with the doctor, the tape recorder was kept in
full view on my knee. From the moral point of view, the physician's explanation of my identity was not true. However, it was
the doctor's own strategy to cooperate with my aim of collecting
spontaneous data. He must have thought that a salesperson would
feel at home and speak freely after hearing that the stranger in
the doctor's office was one of his relatives or close friends.
The doctor also must have thought that if he did not pay much
attention to my presence in his office, the salesperson would
not be disturbed by the stranger's presence. Therefore, the
doctor said nothing about my presence as a response to the
salesperson's question. The encounter situations were artifi-
cially arranged but, as the salesperson concentrated on the
purpose of his visit, he seemed to forget my presence completely
and his talk began to flow naturally, accompanied by body
motions such as repeated bows and nodding.

2.4   Method of collecting data in the United States.
Field work in the United States was carried out in the Washington, Maryland, and Philadelphia areas. As I had done in Japan,
I visited private stores, 'flea markets', department stores, and
hospitals to collect raw data. In Japan, I simply entered the
crowd of people in the stores and on the streets where the
transactions were being held and attempted to collect data.
However, the situation in the United States was totally different.

In the stores and department stores, I was always conscious of
the strange looks I received from people, and of their notice-
ably uneasy attitude. It was my intention to collect raw data
within natural situations but once I began observing the sales
transactions being carried on next to me, another salesperson
would inevitably approach me and inquire, *May I help you?*
Therefore, the next method employed was to obtain permission
from store supervisors. However, in many instances I had

difficulty getting permission to do my research in some places (department stores and drug stores). Even if I succeeded in obtaining permission, many salespeople were very reluctant to have their conversations recorded.

As a result of repeated experiences of this type, I concluded that: (1) since I am obviously a foreigner with marked Oriental looks and behavior patterns, Americans may have been suspicious and curious about my very evident interest in the transactions taking place, and (2) American people seem to be generally more opposed to having their speech recorded than are the Japanese. I therefore attempted a different method. I would accompany my friends to stores and try to collect data while standing next to them. Sometimes, my friend herself was a customer and, at other times, my friend(s) and I were just observers. In this way, a considerable amount of data was collected at department stores, 'flea markets', and private stores.

As to data collected in the hospital, I followed this procedure:

(1) I wrote letters to two different hospitals (both in Washington), explaining the purpose of my research to the administrators.

(2) In one hospital, after meeting the supervisor personally, I was introduced to 'buyers' whose profession is to purchase medical, surgical, and office supplies from salespeople who visit the hospital regularly at least twice a week.

(3) I again explained about my research to the buyers and they promised to cooperate in the project. In the first hospital, there were two buyers and I was permitted to take a place beside each buyer before the salesperson entered the office. Since the setting was informal and both buyers knew most of the salespeople, they seemed to enjoy their conversation after the buyer explained why I was there. However, there were some occasions when it was apparent that the salesperson was tense and ill at ease. This happened usually when the relationship between buyer and salesperson was in its initial stage and they did not yet know each other very well. However, once the salesperson initiated his business and began explaining about new drugs, emphasizing their advantages, and demonstrating how to use surgical supplies, he returned to his own natural mode of speaking and seemed comfortable throughout the remainder of the conversation.

In the second hospital, the drug salesperson had already been informed by the pharmacist, the usual buyer, that I was coming on that day and that the conversation would be taped. Therefore, it was obvious that his talk had been prepared because it was so fluent and well structured, with no repetitions or stammering. The accuracy of this observation was verified by the salesperson in question after the transaction was concluded.

The most difficult task in the United States field work was collecting data regarding door-to-door salesmanship. In addition to the fact that this sales transaction was of a different nature from the rest of the transactions considered here, I learned in the course of interviews with people that in some states there is a law that door-to-door salespeople cannot visit each house. The circumstance naturally made it more difficult to gather data of this type.

After several attempts to obtain a reliable source, I finally succeeded in contacting a door-to-door saleswoman who sells cosmetics. She informed me that she does not visit each house in a given neighborhood, but rather goes to specific places through invitations from friends, family friends, or acquaintances. I invited her to my own place and she agreed after hearing about my research project. I publicized the cosmetic demonstration and sale, and seven friends expressed interest in attending. From the beginning, there was no tension in the group, since all of these prospective customers knew the saleswoman personally. This sales talk turned out to be the longest one among the data collected for this project. It lasted from 8:30 p.m. till 10:20 p.m., from the initial greeting to the end of the social hour that followed the actual demonstration.

Thus, in the United States, the methods of collecting data were as follows: (1) I selected at random several places where I thought I could collect data and I carried out the field work alone; (2) I collected data in the company of American friends who either were real customers or pretended to be prospective customers; (3) I invited a door-to-door salesperson to my home, collecting data generated during the transactions.

After several months of field work in the United States, data had been collected from the following types of transactions: (1) institutional sales, (2) door-to-door sales, (3) department store sales, (4) sales in private stores, (5) sales on the street, and (6) sales at 'flea markets'. The only type lacking, compared with the data collected in Japan, is sales made on trains.

2.4.1 Equipment and recording background. As in the field work in Japan, SONY Casette-Corder TC-1100B was used throughout the collection of raw data in the United States. This was very convenient for recording especially at private stores, department stores, and 'flea markets', since the size of the recorder is comparable to that of a paperback book. For this reason, many people were unaware that a tape recorder was being used. When salespeople were conducting their business with customers in hospitals and other institutions, the tape recorder was placed either on my knee or on the desk. The recorder was visible to some salespeople during the whole conversation and sometimes they looked at me questioningly, but once they understood the reason why I was there, they seemed not to mind the recordings. At the initial encounter, no salesperson asked the buyer about my identity. Usually, it was the buyer who initiated the conversation, explaining the stranger's presence. I believe that salespeople refrained from asking about my identification since I am a foreigner. In this situation, as was also true in Japan, it was a buyer, e.g. a doctor in Japan, who explained the presence of an outsider during the business transaction.

As the foregoing description of the method of collecting data implies, these methods were not totally consistent in both speech communities. The adaptations that had to be made were due to cultural differences, a fact which, in itself, is interesting from an ethnographic perspective.

2.5 Data gathering techniques. As the topic for this investigation is of an anthropological and sociolinguistic nature, data containing actual transactions between salespeople and customers were essential. In addition, background information about selling and buying from both salespeople and customers is also of great importance for the valid analysis and interpretation of data in ethnographic research. This background information often contains pertinent facts about the societal frame in which language exists, and therefore frequently validates and affirms the findings based on the raw data. I used the following three techniques: (1) participant observation, (2) interview with salespeople, and (3) questionnaires. Each technique is discussed here in detail.

2.5.1 Participant observation. While engaged in field work for this research in Japan, I used the technique of participant observation. Except for 17 examples obtained from the Sales Training Center in Tokyo, I was physically present each time during the actual transactions. I observed and took notes about nonverbal behavior (e.g. physical distance between the salesperson and the customer, facial expression, eye contact, nodding and gestures, etc.) while the verbal interaction was being recorded. On some occasions, while facing the salesperson in the role of customer, I made some inquiries and responses and thus entered the actual transaction. This technique was used when I found myself as a customer in private food stores and groceries. However, on other occasions, I was one individual among a number of prospective customers and, as some customers occasionally do, I responded, if requested, to the salesperson's selling demonstrations.

Data were collected mainly in the Tokyo area but when I visited my parents' home in Yokkaichi City, about 225 miles from the capital, I became a real customer and entered, at my mother's request, into actual transactions for the purchase of food and groceries. I believe that the technique of participant observation I used in Japan had some advantages. First of all, because the transactions between salespeople and customers were always visible to me, I observed not only verbal interaction but also nonverbal activities of the participants. Second, since I am an insider in the Japanese speech community, it is not likely that salespersons, customers, or other participants tried either to upgrade or downgrade their speech patterns in my presence.

However, in the case of drug salespeople, in spite of the strategy attempted by the doctor to create a natural situation, some problems have persisted. In Japanese society, a physical doctor is usually called *Sensei*, an honorific form to show respect, and he usually is the object of much esteem. I was concerned that this kind of personal behavior toward a member of this highly respected profession might be elevated in the presence of a third party. More specifically, if a salesperson initially has great respect toward a doctor and moreover is given to understand that the third party is the physician's close friend or relation, he may increase his demonstrations of respect and honor by employing an even more elevated speech style. On the basis of this social behavior characteristic of Japanese people, I think that the preferable way to observe this transaction would have been with the aid of a one-way mirror while simultaneously recording.

In the United States, most of the time I was not a participant in the sales transaction but was exclusively an observer. The reason why I utilized this technique consistently is that, not being a member of the target social group, I thought it more appropriate to observe and record transactions between salespeople and customers belonging to the same speech community. Given the racial and social class diversity characteristic of American society as a whole, decisions were necessary in the selection of the population to be studied. In order to minimize the participant variables involved, I focused on transactions within the middle-class white segment of the American speech community; all recorded sales events and all interviews involved white informants only. The written questionnaires solicited no information regarding race, and distribution of these questionnaires was sometimes in the hands of departmental supervisors rather than being directly administered by the researcher myself. Therefore, some of the information in these written responses may have been from non-Caucasian informants.

2.5.2. Interview. The second technique used in this research was the personal interview with salespeople. All interviews were personally conducted by me both in Japan and in the United States. The purpose of the interview was to elicit background information about salesmanship in general. The questions raised by the interviewer and the topics discussed during the interview generally followed these five categories: (1) basic principles of salesmanship, (2) personal professional qualities, (3) sales techniques and strategies, (4) sales procedures, (5) speech pattern and usage. Sample questions are given in Appendix 1. In Japan, the investigator had interviews with 12 salespersons selected at random. Information regarding types of salespersons and the commodities they sell, as well as their attributes, are shown in Table 2.1.

Table 2.1 General information about Japanese interviewees.

Inform-ant	Sex	Age	Years' experience	Type of sale	Commodity for sale	Location
1	M	60	28	store	men's clothing	Tokyo
2	F	58	30	store	cosmetics	Yokkaichi
3	F	40	20	store	cosmetics	Tokyo
4	M	35	13	store	electrical supplies	Yokkaichi
5	M	22	15	store	electrical supplies	Yokkaichi
6	M	23	5	institutional	drugs	Yokkaichi
7	M	27	4	institutional	electrical supplies	Tokyo
8	M	65	24	store	eye glasses	Yokkaichi
9	M	30	7	institutional	medical supplies, drugs	Nagoya
10	M	32	9	institutional	medical supplies, drugs	Nagoya
11	M	56	35	door-to-door	car	Tokyo
12	F	43	20	store	clothing	Tokyo

The time span for each interview varied from 20 to 75 minutes, with the average time of all interviews being between 40 and 45 minutes. Although I prepared sample questions in advance for each interview, when a particular informant showed special interest in a specific topic, I left the informant free to talk. In fact, one informant spent 40 minutes discussing his own image of a salesperson before moving on to the next topic. All the interviews were carried out with one salesperson at a time and without third party presence or intervention.

The general procedure of the interview was as follows: (1) my explanation of the study, (2) background questions to salesperson, e.g. type of sale and merchandise being sold, etc., and (3) sample questions and responses. During each interview, I asked if the informant objected to having conversation recorded and none seemed to be reluctant. I took notes occasionally to remind myself of remarks of special interest while the tape recorder was in operation. The locations of the interviews are shown in Table 2.1, but locus of the interviews varied and included the following five places: (1) cafeteria, (2) stores, (3) hospital, (4) my brother's home, and (5) my home. Informant 1, after hearing my explanation about the intentions and purpose of the research, took me into a cafeteria near his store and the interview was held with soft background music in an informal situation. This informant showed great interest in the research, since he himself had visited the United States several times on business and had attended workshops sponsored by an American manufacturer of bluejeans. He said:

The American salespeople I know are very friendly and they know how to approach people. One of the things we have to learn from them is how to create a friendly atmosphere with customers at the early stage of greeting in the interaction.

The interviews with informants 2, 3, 4, 5, 8, 11, and 12 were carried out in the stores where they were selling the merchandise. Informant 6, a drug salesperson, happened to appear at the hospital owned by my uncle, an oculist, when I was visiting there. This salesperson agreed to an interview with me and the interview was held in one of the employees' offices. No one else was present and after the salesman had heard that I am the niece of the doctor in charge, he became very friendly and shared many anecdotes of his happy and unhappy experiences as a drug salesman. The most impressive and unexpected statement was the following:

I visit two or three hospitals a day. I stay usually for about one hour and a half in one place. But I spend only 10 or 15 minutes on business. I spend the rest of the time talking and chatting about the doctor's hobbies and about topics of importance in today's world. In doing so, I think I can keep a good human relationship with the doctor. Therefore, I spend a lot of time studying in various fields, for example the field of each doctor's hobbies, like sports, 'bonsai' (Japanese planting arranged on a small pod), or literature.

Informants 9 and 10 were also drug salesmen and they had interviews with me at my brother's house. They usually visit the hospital where my brother, a heart surgeon, is a member of the staff. My brother invited the informants to his home and scheduled the two interviews at separate times. The interview was conducted in the reception room, with only the interviewer and salesperson present. Both of these interviewees expressed opinions similar to that of informant 6, quoted earlier. According to informant 9:

One of the most important techniques in my profession is how to be recognized by the doctors as a good salesperson. So, in addition to studying our own products, I'm always seriously concerned about maintaining a good relationship with a doctor so that I can discuss current events occurring in the medical field but also in the fields of sports, movies, etc.

The interview with informant 7 was held at my home in Tokyo. He explained for more than 20 minutes about how to greet customers and negotiate with them. All through this talk, he emphasized that the spirit of service and respect toward customers are essential qualities of salespeople.

In the United States I had 11 interviews, each time with a different salesperson selected at random. The time spent on each interview was between 30 and 70 minutes and the average time was 40 minutes. The questions raised by the interviewer and the procedures were the same as those employed in the interviews in Japan. Table 2.2 details the information. The loci of

Table 2.2 General information about American interviewees.

Inform-ant	Sex	Age	Years' experience	Type of sale	Commodity for sale	Location
1	F	32	6	institutional	books	Washington, D.C.
2	M	29	6	institutional	books	Washington, D.C.
3	F	63	35	door-to-door	insurance	Washington, D.C.
4	M	28	3	store	car	Philadelphia
5	M	68	22	direct	insurance	Philadelphia
6	F	62	18	store	clothing, flatware	Philadelphia
7	M	34	5	store	printing	Washington, D.C.
8	M	30	4	store	printing	Washington, D.C.
9	F	42	4	door-to-door	cosmetics	Washington, D.C.
10	F	55	30	store	cosmetics	Washington, D.C.
11	M	55	30	store	medical supplies, drugs	Washington, D.C.

the interviews were as follows: (1) a university campus in Washington, D.C. (with informants 1 and 2), (2) a college campus in Washington, my residence (with informants 3 and 9), (3) a friend's house in Philadelphia (with informants 5 and 6), (4) stores (with informants 4, 7, 8, and 10), and (5) a hospital (with informant 11).

Each interview was carried out without third party presence or intervention. Most of the informants, except 7 and 8, emphasized that they make great efforts from the initial encounter to build a good relationship and friendly atmosphere. One of the techniques they use to create this friendly atmosphere, according to informant 1, is:

> First thing I do is try to remember the name of the customer. In my case, I visit professors' offices so I try to address them by their names, usually Dr. so and so, or Professor so and so.

She also mentioned another technique to create a good atmosphere at the initial stage of their encounter, as follows:

> I make comments about something on the wall if they have pretty pictures. Or: Is this your family? What a lovely office! Or gee, it's really a nice office. I try to create the atmosphere of making them comfortable with me.

Informant 3 explained that he sends a birthday card besides business letters to the customers to communicate his appreciation of their patronage and maintain a good relationship. Thus, both in Japan and the United States, each interview was held in an informal atmosphere and each interviewee shared his/her own philosophy of selling, techniques, and strategies with me.

At this point, I would like to interject into the narrative these considerations which I deem essential for the proper understanding of the material presented in Section 2.5.2 and Section 2.5.3. Although similar questions were raised in both the interview and the questionnaire techniques, I am convinced that each of these techniques should be considered a distinct source of information for the following reasons: (1) setting-- since the interview is normally carried out in face-to-face interaction, the points of special interest to interviewer and interviewee may be more fully explored; (2) scope--in an interview, the interviewee has the opportunity for more abundant and spontaneous sharing than would normally be elicited by a written questionnaire. In addition, I would like to point out that the manner in which the interviews were conducted in each of the two target speech communities emphasizes the cultural differences between these two societies.

In Japanese society, the interviewer feels obliged to offer some gifts to show appreciation for the informant's cooperation. For example, my family urged me to prepare an appropriate gift or they themselves offered a present to salespeople who cooperated in the research. In American society, there seems to be no similar expectation or obligation of reward. The interview within the American speech community seems to be a more enjoyable cooperative effort and the interviewees seem eager to contribute their experiences as part of a joint educative effort.

2.5.3 Questionnaires. The third technique I used was that of questionnaires whose purpose was to obtain additional background information from salespeople and customers. I composed questionnaires for salespeople tentatively after consulting sociological references. After the general outline was made, I enlisted the help of two salespeople, both Americans, to evaluate the completeness and pertinence of the tentative questionnaire. Informant A reacted: 'I think it's quite well done, I think I do, I really like this.' Informant B suggested the addition of some items which she thought necessary. After revising a few items, the final format of the questionnaire was completed. The sample questions are indicated in Appendix 2.

The questionnaire consists of six parts: (1) general information about the respondent, e.g. age, sex, types of sales, years of experience, and educational background; (2) examination of salespersonship; (3) qualities and skills as salesperson; (4) sales technique, including how to initiate sales transactions, how to negotiate with customers, and how to close sales; (5) use of address forms and speech patterns; and (6) sales attitudes. Questions in the first three categories are objective questions which the respondent could answer simply by choosing one response from a number of responses listed or by checking one point on the five-point scale. Questions concerning sales techniques and strategies and speech patterns as well as sales attitudes are open-ended questions to which the respondent could reply with a few sentences or a few paragraphs. In regard to the method of convincing the customer to buy, salespeople were asked to assign priorities to a list of variables by numerical indication, e.g. placing 1 before the item they thought most important, 2 for the next in importance, etc.

After the salesperson's questionnaire was completed, the next task was to devise a questionnaire for customers. The purpose was to examine and obtain information about salesmanship from the customer's point of view. Since any sales transaction is composed of interaction between salespeople and customers, I believe that the customer's mentality and philosophy of selling and buying are also influential and affect the principles of salesmanship in each society. The general outline of the customer's questionnaire has four categories:

(1) General information--customer's age and sex
(2) Interaction with salesperson:
    (a) the way to receive a salesperson at home
    (b) how to make contact with him/her
    (c) order of priorities among variables in purchasing products
    (d) how to decline a purchase verbally
    (e) how to take leave
    (f) how to use address forms
(3) Activities after the speech event:
    how to keep in contact with the salesperson if the customer indicates that contact is maintained
(4) Evaluation and attitudes toward salesperson:
    (a) how to define salesperson's identity
    (b) qualities as salesperson

The customers were asked to give objective answers by simply checking the items they thought appropriate or placing numbers according to the order of priorities among variables. They were also requested to supply some essay-style answers to open-ended questions. However, most of the questions were objective questions except (e) under item (2) (concerning the way of taking leave) and item (3) (referring to activities after the sales transaction is over), and the first part of item (4) (in relation to salesperson's status and definition). All the sample questions are included in Appendix 3.

After these two kinds of questionnaires were completed, I translated the English versions into Japanese for use in my field work in Japan. During my stay in Japan, I received 72 completed questionnaires and by December 1979, 22 more questionnaires arrived from the salespeople who were selected by me, my family, friends, and acquaintances. Seventy of the customer questionnaires were returned before I left Japan late in August 1979, and 23 more were mailed to me by the end of 1979.

In the United States, it was rather difficult to find 100 salespeople and ask them to answer the questionnaires, since the circle of my friends in this country is relatively limited. Moreover, I wanted to receive responses from a wide spectrum of salespeople selling many different commodities. Therefore, I went to difference places, e.g. department stores, private stores, and hospitals, and explained about my research to the supervisors of the stores or to someone in an administrative position. Even if they agreed to try to help me by encouraging their employees to fill out the questionnaires, very few salespeople responded to the questionnaires. A typical return would be four questionnaires out of ten. I also asked help from my friends in Boston and Philadelphia. When I was visiting Philadelphia, a friend took me to various places and asked the supervisors to listen to my request. The head of the personnel division in one of the large department stores showed interest in the research and informed me that he would ask the top ten salespeople in that store to fill out the questionnaires. He also asked me to let him know the summary of the answers I received after all the questionnaires were returned to me. By means of several tryouts, going back and forth to the same hospitals, to various stores and department stores, I finally obtained 85 completed questionnaires. Some questionnaires were also returned from Boston, New York, and Philadelphia. Of the completed questionnaires, 83.7% were filled out by women customers.

2.6   Method of transcribing data. After raw data were collected from the Japanese and American speech communities, I undertook another time-consuming task, the transcribing of taped conversations of salesmen. For the purpose of this study, I dismissed phonological variation. Raw data collected in the Japanese speech community were transcribed into Japanese after repeated listening and then translated into English. English raw data were transcribed with the aid of an American friend, since English is not my native language.

2.6.1   Conventions used in transcription. In transcribing the tapes, the following conventions were used:

(1)   The point at which one participant's utterance is interrupted by another speaker is indicated by a double slash.

(2)   The point at which overlapping ends is indicated by an asterisk.

(3)   Parts of inaudible utterances are shown by parentheses. If the investigator has a partial idea as to what the participant was saying, the conjectured utterance is indicated in the parentheses.

(4) Pauses longer than one second were marked by parentheses, with the presumed number of seconds inside the parentheses.

(5) Actions during conversation, sounds made, and some other distinctive manifestations of nonverbal behavior are described in the parentheses.

In addition to these conventions, the following symbols were used in the Japanese versions:

(6) Honorific expressions and usage are marked by the symbol H in parentheses at the conclusion of the word or expression.

(7) Humble forms are marked by the symbol HM in parentheses at the conclusion of the word or expression.

(8) Formal style of speech is indicated by the symbol F in parentheses at the conclusion of the utterance.

2.7 Basic unit of analyzing data. Whatever the nature of linguistic investigation, it is essential to decide the basic unit before attempting a description and analysis of the spoken text.

In several works by Labov (1972), Sacks (1972a), Schegloff (1972), and Jefferson (1972), utterance is treated as the basic unit of analysis. Other linguists, e.g. Bellack, Sinclair and Coulthard, propose that there is a smaller unit than utterance, which they call 'move'.

Even though the proposed theory does not provide precise criteria to define a boundary within the utterance, I believe that it is very useful to work on a category smaller than utterance. The majority of studies which have been done in this field so far have dealt with simple or occasionally regularized or hypothetical data. In a certain type of salesperson's conversational patterns, however, there is a great diversity of speech units within a single utterance, due to the varying intention of the speaker. For example, within a single utterance, it is not difficult to find varieties of functions, e.g. soliciting, introducing, explaining, persuading, negotiating, and so forth. For this reason, I utilize 'move' as a descriptive unit of discourse within the following definition and framework: a 'move' is a minimum functional unit of speech. It may be coextensive with utterances in some cases, but basically it is a unit to describe speech according to the different intentions and functions of speech during the flow of conversation. Examples of 'moves' are found in the analyses in Chapter 3.

CHAPTER THREE

ETHNOGRAPHIC DESCRIPTION OF SALES TRANSACTIONS IN AMERICAN AND JAPANESE SPEECH COMMUNITIES

3.0 Introduction. Data have been categorized according to the types of salespersons who participated in the transactions and the classes of merchandise offered for sale, and then analyzed according to the basic components proposed by Hymes. Four representative events are discussed here, illustrating three different categories: (1) an institutional sale in the American speech community, (2) an institutional sale in the Japanese speech community, (3) a sale in a department store in the American speech community, and (4) a door-to-door sale in the Japanese speech community.

3.1 Analysis of data collected. From the analysis of the 244 events collected within the Japanese speech community, there emerge two general categories of salespersons: (1) those engaged in face-to-face negotiation with prospective customers, and (2) those engaged in a predominantly one-way address to a general audience. The first of these two categories includes salespersons involved in the following transactions: (1) institutional sales, (2) door-to-door sales, (3) sales in a department store, (4) sales in private stores, (5) sales in a market, and (6) sales by street hawkers. The other category includes salespersons involved in using public address systems: (1) in markets, (2) in department stores, and (3) on trains. Table 3.1 illustrates the distribution of the total data base of 244 events according to the types of salespersons involved and the types of merchandise offered.

From the analysis of the 85 events collected within the American speech community, three categories emerge: (1) salespersons engaged in face-to-face negotiation with prospective customers, (2) salespersons engaged in a predominantly one-way address to general audiences, and (3) sales transactions by telephone. The first of these three categories includes salespersons in the following transactions: (1) institutional sales, (2) door-to-door sales, (3) sales in department stores, (4) sales in private stores, (5) sales in drug stores, (6) sales in a flea market, and (7) sales on the street by street hawkers. The second

Table 3.1 Data collected in Japanese speech community.

Merchandise: Types of sales:	Drugs & medical supplies	Food	Advertising	Office & school supplies	Clothes	Sports goods	Flowers	Insurance	Cars	Electric appliances	Cosmetic & household supplies	Magazines an newspapers	Stock market	Number of events observed
1. Institutional	16													16
2. Door-to-door			1	5				4	8	2			3	23
3. Department		1									4			5
4. Private stores	101			1							52			154
5. Markets		11			3					2	2			18
6. Street-hawkers		2					2			1	1			6
7. Public address in the markets		1				1				1	1			4
8. Public address in the department stores					4									4
9. Public address on the train		7										7		14
Number of events recorded:	117	22	1	6	7	1	2	4	8	6	60	7	3	244

category includes salespersons involved in using public address systems in the flea market. The third category includes transactions by telephone between salesperson and customer. The data from this third category are not further analyzed for the following reason: 17 events of this type were collected during research at W hospital in Washington, D.C. Both of the buyers' officers in this hospital are equipped with a special type telephone. A microphone attachment on each buyer's desk made both parts of the telephone conversation audible throughout the office. In the intervals between receiving salespeople in the offices, the buyers frequently activated the microphone by pushing a button on the base of the telephone and placed orders with drug companies and with companies dealing with medicines, surgical, and office supplies. The third party (that is, I) was able to hear clearly both parties, the addressee and the addresser, during the sales transaction. Even if the data collected in this situation were telephone sales transactions, it was always a buyer who initiated and maintained the active part of the conversation with the salesperson, and a salesperson always secured an order automatically. In this respect, these data are somewhat different from the rest of the data collected in both speech communities. While this type of conversation has a definite structure and the data are very interesting and significant for further investigation, they have been excluded from the present study as not being pertinent to its central purpose.

Table 3.2 Data collected in American speech community.

Merchandise:	Drugs & medical supplies	Decorations & accessories	Food	Office & school supplies	Clothes	Cosmetics	Gift & wrapping items	Candy	Housekeeping supplies	Incense, balloons	Number of data collected
Types of sales:											
1. Institutional	7		1	10							18
2. Door-to-door						1					1
3. Department stores				1	6	4	7	1			19
4. Private stores				1					1		2
5. Drug stores				2					1		3
6. Flea markets		3							11		14
7. Street-hawkers		2	1						1	3	7
8. Public address in the flea market		3	1								4
9. Telephone order conversation	17										17
Number of events observed:	24	8	3	14	6	5	7	1	14	3	85

Table 3.2 illustrates the distribution of the 85 events recorded in the United States, according to the criteria of types of salespersons and types of merchandise offered.

Before presenting a general picture of the sales transactions, I would like to make the following comments for the purpose of clarification. The framework of analysis is modeled on the general outline suggested by Hymes. However, for this specific study, some revisions and adaptations have been made: (1) two components, setting and participants, are explained under one heading; (2) for a clearer understanding of the total transaction, the sequence of speech acts is reported verbatim after the general background of the speech event has been provided; (3) since all the data of salesmen's talk to be described in this chapter belong to a specific genre, there is no further identification of the genre component; (4) analysis at the speech act level includes discussion of both code and norms of interpretation and interaction; and (5) at the end of the explanation of individual speech acts or moves, explication of the whole event is given (1) first in terms of the narrative structure and (2) by a chart which presents a more abstract diagram of the structure of each speech event. The data from the Japanese speech community have been translated into English. All of the original Japanese data are available in (a) a series of casette tapes (SONY Casette-Corder TC-1100B), (b) a Japanese transcription in the Hiragana, Katakana, and Kanji alphabets, and (c) a Rōmaji transcription of the Japanese characters. Interested persons may write to the Librarian, Notre Dame Seishin University, 2-16-9, Ifukucho, Okayama, 700 Japan.

3.2 An institutional sale in the American speech community

3.2.1 Setting and participants. The following speech event took place on December 4, 1979, at 10:40 a.m. at G hospital in Washington, D.C. Participant 1 (hereafter S) is a drug salesman who pays a regular visit to this hospital at least once a week. S is in his thirties. Participant 2 (hereafter C) is a pharmacist in her thirties. S wore a dark blue suit and C was in a white pharmacist coat. The conversation began in C's office. S's and C's spatial orientation was close, since C's office is about 10 x 7 square feet. C was sitting at the desk and welcomed S.

3.2.2 Purpose. The expected purposes were for S to check the inventory requested by C, to arrange future business with C, and explain to C's supervisor about a new drug.

3.2.3 Key. S and C have known each other for a couple of years so their relationship is mutually friendly. In the flow of conversation, functional gestures such as surprise and unexpectedness, rising and dropping intonation, and laughter were observed by the researcher.

3.2.4 Act sequence.

1 S: How're you doing? I'm with U company.
2 C: OK. Here is some. Taking inventory. And I'm going to mark down.
3 S: (2) No, no. (waves his right hand)
4 C: What we need.
5 S: You learn a lot in this place. You really do. David and his weekly.
6 C: Oh, yeah. You saw the one about Senator Kennedy?
7 S: Yea, that's the one who told me today.
8 C: OK. I got copies of it (shoves a sheet of paper to S).
9 S: Oh, no. I didn't see that (3). He gave me the one about ( ). You know you got that invoice. Did you see that, Debby?
10 C: Yeah, but it didn't have a price on it, Terry. Just had marks...
11 S: (   )
12 C: Oh, yeah I just had that out there this morning. I was going to mark it. It came in yesterday's mail but we didn't get one copy with the shipment.
13 S: OK. This is the ( ). Will this do?

14 C: Yeah.
15 S: It will do. OK.
16 C: No, I just mean I got a packing slip with what came
        in. We usually get the top copy of the invoice. Did
        you bring it in? I thought you brought it in.
17 S: No.
18 C: (3) that's what happens when you bring it in.
19 S: I placed the order on Thursday. No, I placed the
        order last Wednesday. I placed it Wednesday afternoon.
20 C: H'm, h'm.
21 S: You were just about ( ) of (product's name).
22 C: H'm, h'm.
23 S: And Dick really didn't care (3). He just placed the
        order, he didn't care ( ). I was afraid if we shipped
        it Thursday which would probably happen you wouldn't get
        it until Monday and you would be out of (product's
        name).
24 C: Well we're out of (another product's name).
25 S: So what I did (4) I told the people at the warehouse
        to put a rush on it and they shipped it out that
        afternoon.
26 C: Right.
27 S: And they couldn't get the invoice in the box.
28 C: Right.
29 S: Betty didn't say they promised it?
30 C: No. She says it's been sitting out there. I just
        ( ). He wants to check it off on the invoice to make
        sure the invoice matches it entirely.
31 S: Oh, I know that// (A third party, S2 comes in. S2,
        another drug salesperson, speaks to C.)
32 S2: See you, Debby.
33 C: OK. Stew, take care.
34 S: OK. Here it is again (shows a paper to C). No
        problem, right?
35 C: No problem.
36 S: Otherwise it looks like we're in pretty good shape,
        Deb.
37 C: OK. You come two more times before Christmas?
38 S: I don't know (5) I might not be in...
39 C: You take off early?
40 S: Well...
        (3)
41 C: OK, the 11th? 18th; and then the 25th, so that's two
        more weeks.
42 S: Actually, I'm only going to be here one more time (3).
        Next week.
43 C: What about the 18th? You're going out of town?
44 S: Well, OK. The 18th, I'll be the 18th. But after the
        18th you realize...
45 C: It's going to be two weeks. Three weeks before you're
        back in.

46 S: That's right. Because the 25th I won't be in and then the next week will be what, the second (3). Stores will be closed on the first and second. Dick is really going to have a look at his inventory (3). A few days after Christmas he better look and see what he has.

47 C: H'm, h'm.

48 S: Are you taking off? Christmas?

49 C: Justa Christmas Eve. Mom and Dad are going to be home.

50 S: You get Christmas Day off?

51 C: Yeah, I mean, but I mean extra. And then New Year's, of course, is a holiday. I'm taking a four-day weekend.

52 S: Is there a buffet on Christmas Eve?

53 C: H'm, h'm.

54 S: The buff-it.

55 C: Yeah, the buff-it. You're counting what's the floor.

56 S: Yeah, you see me do that.

57 C: OK.

58 S: This was like a hundred. I changed it to three (5). So Dick's sick.

59 C: No, I think he's working out of space.

60 S: Is he really?

61 C: He said he has something to do.

62 S: He wants to get it done.

63 C: Before Christmas.

64 S: You can't blame him for that.

65 C: Before the weather gets too bad for the kids to play outside.

66 S: Where is he, in Las Vegas?

67 C: Yeah, he lost all his money last night. But he allowed so much for every couple of days, I think so.

68 S: (   )

69 C: Now he's not gambling much.

70 S: I would like to have seen him today. We have another new drug (product's name).

71 C: Huh, huh.

72 S: It was released a couple of weeks ago, and I saw (person's name) and (person's name) who worked on the drug here at (name of place). And they said they wanted (product name) to get some here in the hospital. Did he mention it? I guess he didn't mention it to you. Wonder if he mentioned it to Dick?

73 C: No, I know there was a question on (product name) yesterday.

74 S: When is Dick coming back?

75 C: Seventh. Monday.

76 S: Debby, you got two of these right here, OK? (shows paper to C).

77 C: OK.

78 S: There was one on the shelf I forgot to write down.

79 C: Someone called yesterday, too and wanted to get (product name).
80 S: Are you kidding me?
81 C: No, they wanted to get (product name).
82 S: (repeat the same product name)? Oh my gosh, they don't make (product name), you can get (another product name).
83 C: I know. (product name S first mentioned).
84 S: Who was that (name of person)?
85 C: I don't know who it was. I told them to call back this afternoon if they needed the papers to fill out for it.
86 S: Sure.
87 C: I just wondered if you...
88 S: Surprise, surprise!
89 C: They're all unit dose now, aren't they?
90 S: Well (2).
91 C: Just a form of unit dose. What?
92 S: Just a form.
93 C: Why?
94 S: Well that's the (2). It's probably the one we sell the most of (2). We didn't sell that much of the 600 ...
95 C: We use a lot of the 300 though. Why don't you (3).
96 S: You see a lot of the 300 because they're right for 600 milligrams.
97 C: Oh, oh.
98 S: You give them two.
99 C: What's the package size on (product name)? Twenty-five?
100 S: Twenty-five.
101 C: So. You're finished for the day?
102 S: That's it (2). I gotta go upstairs and play around a little bit.
103 C: (laughter) OK.

3.2.5 Analysis of speech acts. (1) In the conversation, there can be seen a balanced number of moves: 59 moves by S and 56 moves by C.

(2) First names are used when S and C address each other. First, S begins by calling C *Debby* and as a response C calls S *Terry*. During the conversation, S even calls C by a second diminutive, *Deb*.

(3) First name is also used by both S and C when they refer to C's superior as *Dick*.

(4) Except for the use of the first name, the conversation does not have a definite differentiation of male and female speech patterns.

(5) Informal style is predominantly used by both S and C: S uses the following expressions which characterize informal speech.

Utterance (hereafter: U) 80:   Are you kidding me?
U 82:   Oh, my gosh.
U 88:   Surprise, surprise!
U 102:   I gotta go upstairs and play around a little bit.
C uses elliptical sentences such as the following:
U   2:   Taking inventory.
U   4:   What we need.
U 49:   Justa Christmas Eve.
U 55:   Yeah, the buffit.
(6) S's and C's informal style is also marked by rather frequent use of *OK*: 5 times by S and 8 times by C. Each time, that expression carries a specific function. The use and its function by the participants are listed in Table 3.3.

Table 3.3 Use and function of *OK*.

U	Function	C or S
2	Response to greeting	C
8	Marker to urge return to original business	C
13	Consent	S
15	Reaffirmation	S
33	Response to leave-taking	C
34	Marker to suggest return to arrangement	S
37	Agreement and initiates new arrangement	C
41	Suggestion	C
44	Positive answer	S
57	Agreement with foregoing activity	C
76	Request for clarification	C
103	Consent and closing marker	C

(7) Some utterances by S include more than one function, which means they can be further classified into smaller units than utterance, that is, into 'moves'. For example, in utterance 46, S began his exchange of talk about future business arrangements at the end of the year and then switched his conversation to a remark about C's supervisor. Another example is obvious in utterance 58, repeated here.
U 58 S: This was like a hundred. I changed it to three.
          So Dick's sick?
As indicated, S's utterance is composed of at least two moves: (1) discussing inventory, and (2) inquiring about C's superior.

3.2.6   Narrative structure. The conversation began with S's greeting and self-identification. C began her conversation directly about the business topic. However, at intervals within the business talk, S and C share miscellaneous topics like the one about the presidency in regard to Senator Kennedy, planning for vacation, what C's superior is doing, etc. By C's remarks of preclosing, *So. You're finished for the day* (U 101), the actual business conversation was terminated. The interval structure of the whole conversation is diagrammed in Figure 3.1.

Figure 3.1 Structure of an institutional sales transaction in the American speech community.

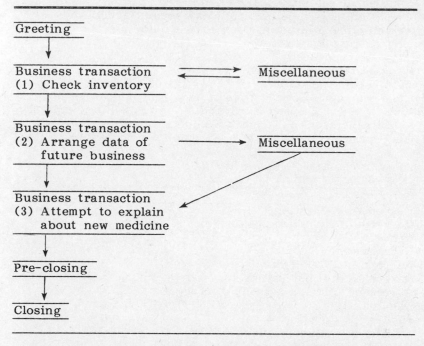

3.3 An institutional sale in the Japanese speech community

3.3.1 Setting and participants.

This conversation took place on July 24, 1979 at 2:30 p.m. at X hospital in Tokyo. S is a drug salesman. He visits C, who is a doctor of internal medicine, at least twice a week. X hospital is a private hospital with numerous departments and C is the head of the department of internal medicine. C is in his fifties and wears a white physician's coat. S is in his late thirties and is in a gray suit. S knocks at C's office after being summoned and opens the door.

3.3.2 Purpose.

The expected purpose was for S to explain the new product and to promote its sale to C. Also, S intends to organize a medical study session sponsored by his own company and to invite C and the other doctors to attend.

3.3.3 Key.

The attitudinal tone is rather ceremonious but not authoritative. Although the social status of the participants is different, C's personality does not force S to behave as an inferior. Therefore, the atmosphere in which the speech event occurs is rather formal but mutually receptive and pleasant.

3.3.4 Act sequence.

1 S: Excuse me, (5) (after the deep bow he shows a surprised look to find the third party (the researcher, R) sitting at the left side of C and says to C): Well, am I interrupting you?

2 C: Oh, no, please. She is one of my relatives so she came to see me here.

3 R: (The researcher looks at S and says) Good afternoon. (S sits on a chair at the right side of C).

4 C: I feel sorry for you because you came (H) first today, didn't you?

5 S: Yes, well (3), because I have been talking (H) with Dr. A (F)...

6 C: Is that so?

7 S: Excuse me (F).

8 C: That's all right.

9 S: Well, I also talked (HM) with Dr. A (H) a moment ago about this matter (F), but how about going out to enjoy the cool of the evening, because it's too hot?

10 C: We will discuss it later, won't we?

11 S: Yes, I heard that you have a lot of meetings in the daytime, therefore (4). (presenting a bottle of pills). This is a sample of (name of medicine) (F). We did not give much information in this hospital (F) but we received a telephone call from the pharmacists' office in this hospital and so (3).

12 C: Well.

13 S: We are very happy to give (HM) P.R. to the doctors in this hospital (F). Is (name of medicine) rotating to a certain degree in this hospital (F) *Sensei* (H)?

14 C: Yes, if we have a patient with heart disease.

15 S: *Sensei*, this medicine is good to use (H) for the patients who suffer from heart trouble, heart arrest (F). In short, this is good for anyone who has symptoms of any kind of shock (F).
(Conversation was interrupted by telephone call. After C answered the phone, S continued.)

16 S: They say that this is very effective for urination ...

17 C: Is that so?

18 S: I would like to leave (HM) this sample here. (S extends his hand and gives the medicine to C.)

19 C: Huh huh.

20 S: Please may I ask you to use (H) this medicine in case of the symptoms I explained?

21 C: Huh huh. This medicine isn't so new, is it?

22 S: Yes, it is only a year ago when it began to sell (H), but we could not afford to give P.R. to this hospital soon (5).

23 C: Rather you didn't do it.

24　S: I should say what you said is right and we have to apologize (HM) for that.

25　C: There are many kinds of shocks caused by heart condition or even viral flu.

26　S: Yes, I understand. I would like you to use (H) this for those occasions (F).

27　C: How can I use it?

28　S: Well, *Sensei*, this is a little bit complicated until we are accustomed to use this (F). (S presents a sheet of paper on which some diagrams are listed.) See, this is an attached calculator (F) and well, on angle is 100 milligrams (F). The below is a quantity for prescription which means a quantity per minute (F). The above is a weight of the patient (F).

29　C: Yes, indeed (5).

30　S: Yes, you can prescribe (H), like (3) suppose the patient is 60 kilograms, this is the quantity of the dissolution (2) (F). If it is 500 cc, this is the way for the hour (F). In short, if you want to use (H) this for the patient weighing 60 kilograms, you will use (H) 1.5 cc dissolution (F).

31　C: Yea, yea.

32　S: It depends on the patient's condition like the condition of blood pressure that you will increase (H) or decrease the dosage of that medicine (F).

33　C: Is that so?

34　S: I can recommend to use (H) it up to 5 gamma (F) and if you use it more that 10 gamma (F) it will be completely ... ( ).

35　C: Yea, 5 gamma is right?

36　S: Yes, but we cannot tell generally that 5 gamma is the best (F). In case of emergency (F), for example, it will be necessary to use the whole on a large scale (F).

37　C: Yes, it will cause the reduction of blood pressure.

38　S: Namely, as you have mentioned (H) before, I would like you to use (H) it in many cases of shock condition like nervous breakdown or heart trouble (F). Also, it is effective for urination (F).

39　C: Is that so? The person is saved. He was a patient suffering from pancreatitis and his condition reduced blood pressure very rapidly...

40　S: Hum, hum.

41　C: At any rate, he almost died.

42　S: Yes.

43　C: Finally, we succeeded in stimulating from urination! ... (5)

44　S: (Nods) If you have such kind of cases (F), please try to use (H) this (F) and I think, even though I have to apologize for saying it (F) this way, it is a good opportunity to evaluate (H) the medicine (F).

45 C: Sometimes, we have to see people dying (F). (3)

46 S: (Nod) Yes, indeed.

47 C: At any rate, recently shock (3). This about an old German lady. Unfortunately, she died (F).

48 S: Please try to use (H) this. (After bow, showing a pamphlet about an academic convention of medicine) I am sure that you already know (H) this. Well, when we had a conference one evening, we invited (H) you as well as all the doctors of internal medicine (F) but many doctors (H) had another engagement (F).

49 C: Do you mean that we all didn't attend?

50 S: Therefore, we talked (H) to the doctors of external medicine (F) and that time, we had (H) Dr. G (H) (F).

51 C: Where was the meeting?

52 S: Where was it that time, I wonder (F)? It was a day when we had heavy rain (F).

53 C: Is that so? You mean that you had that conference outside this hospital?

54 S: Yes, *Sensei* (H), do you have a conference in the hospital once a month (F)? (3)

55 C: You can talk about this matter with the people in the medical office. You can say that you want to explain about the medicine for the stomach, for example.

56 S: Is that so. I will go (HM) to the medical office first (3). In the summer vacation, the second Tuesday (2) Is that day? (3)

57 C: There is no meeting on that Tuesday. Tuesday might be good. Well, maybe, the third Tuesday will be better. Anyway, any Tuesday is all right. Although some people cannot attend some meeting, for example, when they take vacation on that day. However, if someone listens to your explanation, I believe it is still helpful.

58 S: Yes (nods several times).

59 C: Why don't you talk (H) with Dr. M (H)?

60 S: Yes, I will.

61 C: Well, Dr. Y (H) will take the summer vacation. Therefore, you had better check Dr. A's (H) convenience.

62 S: Yes.

63 C: You can ask Dr. D's (H) convenience also. Usually, he only takes vacation during *Obon*.[1] He will visit his ancestors' graves.

64 S: Yes, yes.

65 C: Then why don't you decide finally?

---

1. *Obon* is a special time of reunion for Japanese people. It usually comes in mid-August and many people who are living away from their native place return to the family. The original purpose of the period is also to visit ancestors' graves and pray for the souls of immediate family members.

66 S: Yes, I will.

67 C: I am willing to hear it. It sounds interesting, doesn't it?

68 S: Well, it is much better to ask someone in the academic department of my company rather than to do it myself// (F).

69 C: Indeed,* it sounds a good idea.

70 S: You will understand better.

71 C: Yes.

72 S: *Sensei* (H), if you have this kind of conference, you mean you have (H) it in the afternoon like 5 or 6 o'clock (F)?

73 C: Yes, you know, we are all busy in the daytime.

74 S: Yes, I understand.

75 C: Therefore, I think that we cannot attend before 4:30. Four o'clock is good also. Even 3:30 may be good. Anyway, ask Mr. M when you can have this kind of meeting.

76 S: Yes, I will (F), I will talk to Dr. M (F).

77 C: Huh, huh.

78 S: I am very happy to have (H) this kind of opportunity (F).

79 C: I cannot guarantee the percentage of attendance.

80 S: I am happy even for having (HM) this kind of opportunity (F). In short, this is a very complicated medicine (F), so I have received many questions from the doctors (F). Therefore, it will be a help if someone in the company will answer... (inaudible) (3) By the way, how about (name of medicine)?

81 C: That medicine is very easy to use (F).

82 S: Yes (smiles at C).

83 C: So, I'm using it (F).

84 S: Isn't it possible to order more (F)?

85 C: You mean 2 grams?

86 S: Yesterday, we had a meeting of people who are in charge of hospitals (F). There was a report that national hospitals have 70% ratio of stomach trouble (F).

87 C: Is that so? And they are not reduced?

88 S: No, they aren't.

89 C: Really? (with a surprised look and with singing intonation)

90 S: Therefore the distribution is like 30% ratio of stomach ulcer (F) and 70% ratio of other stomach troubles (F) and they are not reduced (F). Therefore, if we think of the fact that such a big hospital is doing this kind of thing (F), we can admit that the medicine we are using for the stomach ulcer... (F).

91 C: Yes, I think it strange to distinguish between the two.

92 S: Yes, I think so, too (F).

93 C: Well, the doctors are evaluating, aren't they?

94 S: Yes, yes.

95 C: How can they evaluate? There is no way of doing it.
96 S: Yes, therefore, I heard that most of the institution and hospitals are the same in that distribution and in the extreme case, they report 100% stomach trouble (F). However, *Sensei*, there is no problem about that (F).
97 C: Well, then, S hospital will do that. And if they reduce, we request to increase it.
98 S: Yes, there is no problem for that (F).
99 C: Why don't you talk (H) to the doctors (H)?
100 S: So, I will (HM) (F). Please you doctors (H) try to comply with our request (F).
101 C: Yes, I will ask you, too.
102 S: Excuse me but I will visit (HM) you again very soon (F).
103 C: You are welcome until very late.
104 S: Well, *Sochira* (you) (H) or Dr. M (H) will... I will come (HM) and talk (HM) with him soon about that matter (F).
105 C: Yes, it's a good idea to have that kind of meeting only in the department of internal medicine but let's do that in general, anyway.
106 S: Yes, I understand (F). Please comply with my request (F).
107 C: Yes.
108 S: Excuse me (F).
(S stands and gives deep bow to C several times and leaves.)

3.3.5 Analysis of speech acts. (1) The distribution of moves in the conversation is as follows: 67 moves by S and 59 moves by C.

(2) First names are not used when S and C address each other. S calls C either *Sensei* or *Sochira*. *Sensei* 'teacher' is used as an honorific expression of respect. *Sochira* is a polite expression signifying second person singular. C does not use any address form to S.

(3) Honorific usages are employed 32 times by S, and only 8 times by C. S's honorific usages are predominantly employed when he (1) requests something, (2) apologizes for what he didn't do, (3) affirms what C explains, and (4) simply asks C's opinions about relevant topics in the conversation. On the other hand, C uses honorific forms when he (1) apologizes to S for having kept him waiting a long time, (2) gives some suggestions to S, and (3) refers to fellow physicians working in the same hospital.

(4) S's speech is marked by frequent use of honorific forms in formal speech style, while C's speech is characterized by the lack of use of these forms and styles.

(5) S also uses humble forms when he explains (1) about what he did, (2) about what he intends to do, and (3) about himself in general to C.

(6) C's informal speech style is distinguished by rather frequent use of the postpositional particle *ne* at the end of each sentence: 7 times by S and 29 times by C. In general, the functions of the postpositional particle *ne* are indicated as follows:

Function 1: expresses a feeling of indirect judgment.
Function 2: renders a feeling of indirect insistence.
Function 3: asks agreement and answers to questions.
Function 4: asks questions indirectly.
Function 5: emphasizes the expression.
Function 6: serves as a linking marker with the next topic.

Table 3.4 gives a list of functions and distribution of the use of the postpositional particle *ne* employed by S and C.

Table 3.4 Postpositional particle *ne*.

Function of *ne*	Number of times used: By S:	By C:
1	1	6
2	1	7
3	1	2
4	0	1
5	1	5
6	2	8

(7) Some utterances by S can be further classified into moves: utterance 11 consists of two moves; the function of the first move is to present an implicit reason why he prefers to invite the doctors in the evening and not in the daytime. Then he switches his theme to his own business, presenting a sample of a medicine:

U 11 S: Yes, I heard that you have a lot of meetings in the daytime, therefore. This is a sample of (name of medicine). We did not give much information in this hospital but we received a telephone call from the pharmacists' office in this hospital and so...

Similarly, utterance 48 consists of two moves: (1) invitation to C to use the medicine, and (2) explanation about the medical conference.

U 48 S: Please try to use this. (Showing a pamphlet about an academic convention of medicine.) I am sure you already know this. Well, when we had a conference one evening, we invited you as well as all the doctors of internal medicine, but many doctors had another engagement.

3.3.6 Narrative structure. When S entered C's office, he unexpectedly encountered R, the investigator, seated next to C. The conversation began with S's expression of surprise and embarrassment. This part may be called the prelude to the conversation, since it centers on the clarification that puts the participants at ease and establishes an environment of trust in which they can converse pleasantly and freely. After C's well-intended but erroneous story about the identification of the third party, the conversation was continued by C, who apologized for having kept S waiting so long. After S's response to this statement, S offered C an invitation to dinner. Consequently, the conversation related to the real business transaction was not initiated until utterance 11. Then, S's talk centered on the business at hand as follows: (1) the introduction of a new medicine, (2) explanation of its effects, (3) request for the use of the medicine, etc. The second topic for the business transaction was for S to ask C's opinion about the possibility of a medical conference. Then, before closing his conversation, he repeated to C the request to use the medicine. After the apparent expression of preclosing by S, *Excuse me but I will visit you again very soon*, and by C, *You are welcome until very late*, S tried to clarify the procedures for setting up the medical conference. The general outline of the whole conversation is shown in Figure 3.2.

3.4 A department store sale in the American speech community

3.4.1 Setting and participants. The following conversation took place in the first floor cosmetic department of Y department store in Philadelphia on October 24, 1979 at 11:40 a.m. S1 is a salesman who demonstrated Z cosmetic products. He is in his thirties. C1 is a customer in her late fifties. C2 is C1's friend, a woman whose age is 35. S2 is S1's assistant, and she is about 33 years old. S3 is a salesgirl who is at the cash register. S1 wore a dark blue suit and C1 was in a sweater and slacks. C1 and C2 were passing by the cosmetic department. S1 approached C1 and C2.

3.4.2 Purpose. The expected outcome is for S1 to demonstrate a facial using his brand of cosmetics on C1 and to sell the products to C1.

3.4.3 Key. The conversation was carried out principally by S1 and C1, who happened to meet each other where C1 was employed. The attitudinal tone was friendly and pleasant, accom-

Figure 3.2 Structure of an institutional sales transaction in the Japanese speech community.

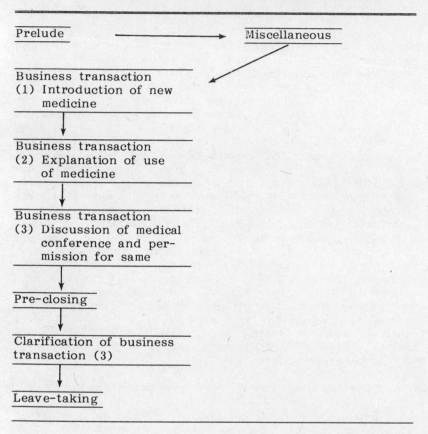

panied by laughter and by S1's sharing of personal episodes with
C1.

3.4.4 Act sequence.

(S1 approaches C1, showing a picture in a cosmetics magazine,
and speaks to C1.)

1 S1: It gives you the look you see in magazines and not
something you don't see. Want to try it?
2 C1: (a little bit hesitant, looks at C2. C2 nods and
then) OK, I'll try it.
3 S1: Take a seat, I'm glad you are here. (Then speaks to
C2) Would you like to have yours? We have another
artist here, Miss Rhodes?

4 C2: No.

5 S1: Take a seat, I'm glad you are here. (Then speaks to C2) Would you like to have yours? We have another artist here, Miss Rhodes?

6 C1: This is the deep cleaner for the skin. Use some skin care--all right? You have baby soft hair. Don't she have silky hair?

7 S1: But, it's nice. It feels like silk. Now, I'm rotating cream around the forehead.

8 C1: Take out the wrinkles of old age?

9 S1: You're not wrinkled very much. You're not that old. A little dry, though the skin. We sold out of our moisturizer, very good moisturizing cream. We'll mark it down low. Have you used (S1's brand name) before?

10 C1: I only use powder and lipstick, but I never use any skin creams.

11 S1: Yum. Well the creams are very very good. They are basic too. They are not a lot of rigmarole. We're rotating into the skin and cleansing deep. Feel how moist? It turned into a liquid then. You know your massage is done. I put always like this.

12 C1: Do away with the double chins?

13 S1: You have a beautiful face so you don't have a chin either you don't have a double chin.

14 C1: No.

15 S1: I have a double chin. I had a picture taken and someone said, 'You have an awful big double chin.'

16 S2: At certain angles, certain angles.

17 S1: That's just part of the family, you know, straight. I knew a movie producer once who wanted to put me in a picture and he wanted me to go see a plastic surgeon. He said to have this cut out. It was my throat. That's true. He say, 'You would have a perfect profile with this cut off.' It's the truth, a friend of Mark's who was doing a movie in New York. We're at a party. Well, I (3) you can't cut your voice box out. I would rather talk than have a good profile. (laugh) Here's the freshener balm.

18 C1: First the moisturizer, then it's the freshener balm?

19 S1: Yeah. It's the freshener to exhilarate the skin. It's not dry. It's real mild too, isn't it?

20 C1: Yes, it doesn't sting.

21 S1: You have a tendency to little capillaries here. Never use anything too strong; or blow your nose too hard. (points to the place) See here. They can be taken off you know.

22 C1: Oh, can they? I never knew I had them. (laugh) That's how much I look at my face.

23 S1: It's a little vein here. A little tiny...right here. You can have that ah ah taken off with an electric needle at a dermatologist. Very easy. It would cost

		you about $15.00.
24	C1:	Oh, really?
25	S1:	(Showing the facial cotton to C1) See this is skin coming off your face. See that, it's little pieces of skin. That's what that does ( ). Can't get away from the music these days, can you? (talking about noisy rock music) Everyone plays that rock music everywhere you go.
26	C1:	What's this? (pointing to a bottle)
27	S1:	Moisturizer. Now you already this is not a line. We're out of this right now. Your skin looks different already, doesn't it? (to C2) Doesn't her skin look more moist?
28	C2:	Yes, it does.
29	S1:	Don't make yourself dry looking. You're a young looking woman. When you put that dry powder all over your face what you do is take a lot of moisture out of your skin. And skin needs moisture. It would be like taking a plant--do you have any plants?
30	C1:	Yes.
		(3)
31	S1:	(...) and putting powder all over them. You'd dry them out. Dust kills plants, too. You understand me?
32	C1:	Yes, you have to clean the leaves off.
33	S1:	That's what you do to your face when you put too much powder. Is that moist?
34	C1:	Yes.
35	S1:	Never look flaked.
36	C2:	Oh, that's nice.
37	S1:	(to C2) Is she lovely?
38	C2:	H'm, h'm.
39	S1:	See the difference in your skin. . It's wonderful. It's a whole new approach.
40	C1:	How about the skin on my forehead?
41	S1:	Well, the powder takes that off. See the powder? Transparent. Now I (3) You get very red, don't you?
42	C1:	Yeah.
43	S1:	You wouldn't use pink rose. You use a brown (1) softer.
44	C1:	No, any kind (1) that's one reason I don't use makeup very much, cause any kind of skin astringent or lotion turns my skin red and I hope I don't have hives.
45	S1:	This didn't burn did it? That freshener?
46	C1:	It burns now (pointing to the nose) here in my nose.
47	S1:	It does?
48	C1:	Right around here.
49	S1:	That's because of the little capillaries. You are its surface veins. It shouldn't burn.
50	C1:	(to C2) Is my face real red?
51	C2:	No.
52	S1:	See a little of the nutmeg (shade of powder) See I

use the brown.

53 C1: Oh!

54 S1: See, the difference.

55 C1: OK.

56 S1: You need some of this rouge for yourself. Some of that blush. You wear makeup?

57 C1: No.

58 S1: Probably want to, though, right? You don't want to use eye shadow.

59 C1: No, not really.

60 S1: (   )

61 C1: I probably would scare myself.

62 S1: No (3). Does she look scared (pointing to C2)?

63 C2: No, (2). She's a young woman.

64 S1: Well, when you start thinking older you look older. Never think of yourself as an older person. Life is too short to get old.

65 S2: (to S1) Wink, what check tone is that?

66 S1: (to S2) Nutmeg. (to C1) How do you feel, OK?

67 C1: OK.

68 S1: The same way I do (4). You never get old. Life is ( ). Just never feel old. Let's give you a little bit of color on your eyes (showing the eye shadow). Here this is a little bit of disguise (3). This may ( ). (Refers to loud background noise.)

69 S2: (to S1) It is enough to make you 'waco'.

70 S1: I can't think straight. See and then the mascara. Have you ever tried a pencil to outline your lips?

71 C1: No.

72 S1: It's a new pencil to outline (3). I guess my appointment will be here in a couple of minutes. (to C2) Isn't she beautiful?

73 C2: H'm, h'm.

74 C1: (to C2) Do you like it?

75 S1: You look lovely. That makeup does justice to your skin. Very nice.

76 C1: Do you give me a list of what he used?

77 S2: H'm, h'm.

78 C2: (to C1) Pretty.

79 S1: What you need is some of this foundation. It's gorgeous on your skin. You notice the difference in the blush? I just say I didn't overpower your eyes (with the mascara). Let me show you how to do that. Come over the counter with me. What you do put the teal in the crease. On your lid is the mother of pearl. That's to highlight it. It's a cream you just put on your lid. It's good for your eyes. It keeps the skin from drying out. And then brown mascara. Also you can put on this highlighter for night time. It's the mother of pearl. Do you want to try some of that foundation, the biege one?

80 C1: No. I want to think about it.
81 S1: You don't want anything? Not even lipstick?
82 C1: No, I think I want to see how this feels for a-while.
83 S1: Well, the lipstick wouldn't hurt you.
84 C1: What kind of lipstick is that?
85 S1: It's tapestry rose. You can wear lipstick. Can't you?
86 C1: Oh, yeah.
87 S1: Why don't you get the lipstick?
88 C1: I mean is that in a tube?
89 S1: In a tube.
90 C1: In a tube. What did you put it on with, a brush?
91 S1: You can use the pencil too. I'll show you the pencil. You don't need a brush.
92 C1: (to C2) Do you have my pocketbook?
93 S1: (to S2) Burgundy pencil and tapestry rose lipstick.
94 S1: (to C1) The lipstick you should have for yourself.
95 C1: Yes, I have lipstick. It's (S1's brand's name), but it's you know the (4).
96 S1: This is in a tube. This is the pencil now. This outline prevents feathering your lip. You know how it feathers sometimes.
97 C1: Yes.
98 S1: This comes in the pencil and then you just pull this off and outline your lips.
99 C1: I see. Yeah, OK.
100 S1: And the lipstick is beautiful and you should come back for these.
101 C1: May I have this? (referring to chart of face)
102 S1: Yeah, that's yours.
103 C1: OK.
104 S1: The lipstick is in a regular tube.
105 C1: Oh, good.
106 S1: It's in a thin tube rather than a wide ( ).
107 C1: Yeah. I always use (S1's brand's name) things.
108 S1: I don't know why you didn't get that rouge. (to C2) Isn't that pretty on her? The blush wouldn't hurt you.
109 C1: (showing her lipstick tube to S1) See this is what I have.
110 S1: (showing his own to C1) See this is beautiful.
111 C1: (again tries to show hers) See this is the one I have.
112 S1: It is too strong a stain for your lips. See your lips how they're drying. You're staining and drying them out. This is a conditioner (2) Is that charge?
113 C1: No, pay.
114 S1: (to S3) She's going to pay cash for these. (3)

		(to C1) You don't want to get your makeup? The blush?
115	C1:	I'm going to think about that. I might be back later.
116	S1:	Not even the blush?
117	C1:	I might be back later.
118	S1:	The powder is transparent.
119	C1:	Yes, yes.
120	S3:	$8.50.
121	S1:	(receives the money from C1 and hands it to S3) Here we are.
122	C1:	OK, fine, thank you.
123	S1:	Now these are your booklets, eyes, lips and face.
124	C1:	I'll look these over.
125	S1:	You should get some of that treatment. I have a lot of it. Here we are.
126	C1:	I'll be back when I know what I want.
127	S1:	(presenting a dry flower with perfume to C1) Here's a flower for you.
128	S3:	(to C1) Do you have a penny? I'll give you a dollar change.
129	C1:	(to S3) A penny did you say?
130	S3:	Yes, with the tax.
131	S1:	(presenting another flower) Here you are.
132	C1:	Oh, thank you.
133	S1:	(to C2) Do you want one of those? (extending a dry flower to C2) It's the new fragrance--flowers.
134	C2:	Oh, thank you (receives the flower) (S1 presents another one to C2)
135	S1:	That's (S1's brand name) new one.
136	C2:	Oh, thank you (receives it). C1 and C2 leave.

3.4.5 Analysis of speech acts. (1) Total number of utterances by S1, C1, C2, S2 and S3 is 136. The distribution of the principal participants (S1 and C1) in the foregoing conversation is as follows: 94 moves by S1 and 55 moves by C1.

(2) When S2 calls S1, she uses S1's first name, but when S1 mentions S2 to C2, he identifies S2 by her family name.

(3) Seven different speech patterns are used by S1 to invite C1 and C2 to buy, as follows:

Pattern 1, U 1:	Want to try it?
Pattern 2, U 79:	Do you want to try some of that foundation, the beige one?
Pattern 3, U 3:	Would you like to have yours?
Pattern 4, (1) U 81:	You don't want anything? Not even lipstick?
(2) U 114:	You don't want to get your makeup?
Pattern 5, U 108:	I don't know why you didn't get that rouge.

Pattern 6, (1) U 94:   The lipstick you should have for yourself.

(2) U 100:   ...and the lipstick is beautiful and you should come back for these.

(3) U 125:   You should get some of that treatment.

Pattern 7, U 87:   Why don't you get the lipstick?

These patterns indicate varying degrees of politeness and directness in S1's sales approach.

(4) S1 uses two kinds of strategies to convince C1 about the notable effect at each stage of C1's facial: (1) by expressing praise and admiration directly to C1 and (2) by seeking C2's support of these opinions, in order to impress C1. Examples of the first technique are:

U 27:   Your skin looks different already, doesn't it?

U 39:   See the difference in your skin. It's wonderful. It's a whole new approach.

U 75:   You look lovely. That makeup does justice to your skin.

U 79:   ...It's gorgeous on your skin. You notice the difference in the blush...

The second technique S1 uses is to ask C2's agreement about his comment and admiration of C1's facial change:

U 27:   Doesn't her skin look more moist?

U 37:   Is she lovely?

U 72:   ...Isn't she beautiful?

U 108:   ...Isn't that pretty on her? ...

(5) When S1 gives instruction to C1 not to dry her skin as a result of putting too much powder on her face, he explains the condition of dry skin, using a metaphor about plants: dust kills plants.

(6) S1 returns no response to C1 after she mentions that she uses S1's brand of cosmetics. Moreover, S1 seems to pay no attention to C1's comments but, instead, continues his own business talk.

(7) S1 offers direct comment regarding the color of the lipstick C1 shows, even though he was not asked to do so explicitly:

U 111 C1: See this is one I have.

U 112 S1: It is too strong a stain for your lips. See your lips how they're drying. You're staining and drying them out...

(8) In contrast to C1's utterances, S1's utterances are composed of moves within single utterances:

U 5:   (1) explanation of skin cleaner.

           (2) comment on C1's hair.

           (3) request agreement from C2 about his comment.

U 7:   (1) praise of C1's hair.

           (2) explanation of skin cream.

U 9:   (1) comment on the nature of C1's facial skin.

           (2) comment on availability and price of moisturizing cream.

           (3) questioning customer's familiarity with product.

U 17:   (1) talking about a personal episode.

           (2) explanation about skin freshener.

U 25:   (1) explanation of the effect of the skin freshener.

           (2) complaint about noisy background music.

U 68:   (1) talking about how to live.

           (2) explanation about the color of eyeshadow.

           (3) complaint about noisy music.

U 70:   (1) complaint about music.

           (2) explanation of mascara.

           (3) asking about lipstick pencil.

U 72:   (1) explanation of the pencil for lipstick.

           (2) statement of meeting with another client.

           (3) questioning to the third party.

3.4.6 Narrative structure. The conversation began with S1's solicitation to try out makeup demonstration. Once C1 accepted S1's invitation, S1 initiated his business talk directly. However, in the course of his business conversation, he interspersed personal episodes and made some remarks with a philosophical touch like the comment, *Never think of yourself as an older person. Life is too short to get old.* Following S1's demonstration on C1's face, he began to persuade C1 to purchase the cosmetics he had used for her facial. After several exchanges of utterances between S1 and C1, C1 finally decided to buy a lipstick. After C1's purchase of lipstick, S1's persuasion continued until the business talk was concluded by C1's utterance, *I'll be back when I know what I want.* There was no statement of gratitude by S1 for C1's purchase but S1 showed his appreciation by presenting a little gift, a fragrance dry flower, to both C1 and C2. Therefore, the final closing of the conversation was the gratitude response to S1's little gifts to C1 and C2, before they left the scene. The whole conversation can be analyzed by the stages in Figure 3.3.

3.5 A door-to-door sale in the Japanese speech community

3.5.1 Setting and participants. S is a salesperson in his forties, selling a sewing machine. C is a housewife, mother of two daughters. The following conversation took place at the door of C's house in Tokyo. For both S and C, this was an initial encounter.

Figure 3.3 Structure of a sales transaction in an American department store.

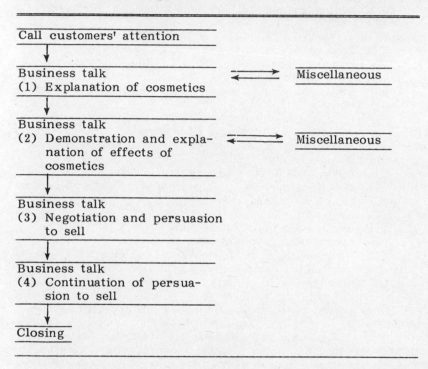

3.5.2 Purpose. The expected purpose of this conversation is for S to sell a sewing machine to C.

3.5.3 Key. The attitudinal tone was not entirely cooperative, especially at the beginning of the conversation, since C had no intention of buying the merchandise S was advertising. Therefore, the spirit in which the speech event began was characterized by coercion on S's part.

3.5.4 Act sequence.

1 S: Excuse me. (F)
2 C: Yes.
3 S: Excuse me (F). I'm from J (company's name) (F). Yes, J (company) (F).
4 C: What do you want of me?
5 S: Do you know, *Okusan* (H) (meaning housewife) about television commercial (F)? The one we can sew even very thick ones or even very thin ones...
6 C: Well, a sewing maching (2). We have one at home.
7 S: Is that so (F)?
8 C: Yes.

9 S: When did you buy (H) it (F)?
10 C: Well, let me think (2). Four or five years ago.
11 S: Four or five years ago. Is that for straight or for zigzag (F)?
12 C: It is for zigzag (F).
13 S: Hum, hum. Zigzag (2). Which (H) brand is that (F)?
14 C: J brand, I wonder.
15 S: Is that so (F)? Thank you so much (F). Is that one which we change *cam* (a part of the machine)?
16 C: What?
17 S: You know about *cam* which is so many attachments?
18 C: Yes.
19 S: About 20 things. I mean you change them. (F)
20 C: Hum.
21 S: The new sewing machine which began selling on May 1 does not need to change *cam* (F). We call it electronic sewing machine.
22 C: We already have one now. It's enough for my house.
23 S: A sewing machine?
24 C: Yeah.
25 S: Yes? A sewing machine? Well, the new one is like this (F) (shows the pamphlet to C). If you want to sew jeans, we can do it 12 (F). ( )
26 C: Is that so? But I don't think we have to sew jeans. We can buy ready-made and we are buying them.
27 S: Yes there are (2). But when you want to open around here (points out the hemming part in the jeans of the picture to C). I think you need to use (H) this at home (H) (F). We have now the other kind (F). (Shows the sample picture of embroidery attachment to C.) You can have these kinds of embroidery (F). It is very popular now, isn't it? We can embroider these kinds also with the old sewing machine. You would have done that but the result looked like a little bit tangled.
28 C: Yes, I can see.
29 S: Especially, because this is very thin (F).
30 C: Therefore, we don't do that at home (2). We usually use ready-made.
31 S: Hum, hum.
32 C: We never make something by ourselves and wear it.
33 S: Hum, hum, hum.
34 C: Therefore, there is no way (3).
35 S: Is that so (F)? Hum, hum. Nowadays, a skirt (2) is very expensive, isn't it (F)? Yes, even if you order it, it's expensive.
36 C: There are many ready-made ones (F).
37 S: Certainly, there are (F).
38 C: The daughter of our family is wearing all ready-made ones (F).
39 S: Hum, hum, hum (2). Then, for your daughter's marriage (H), how about one (F)? If you pay 3,000 yen monthly

		you will get interest of 15%, that is 450 yen (F).
40	C:	I mean we did it before (F). That's why we have one at home.
41	S:	Is that so? Did you get (H) that one by monthly installment (F)?
42	C:	Yeah.
43	S:	It is cheaper (H) if you do monthly installment, isn't it (F)?
44	C:	We don't know if it is cheaper or not. (laughter) Anyway, we were recommended to do so.
45	S:	Hum, hum.
46	C:	We got that. However, we received the machine at the middle of the process of monthly installment.
47	S:	Hum, hum (2). You paid the rest of the money?
48	C:	Hum, hum.
49	S:	Is that so (F)? If you pay a deposit, I can bring (HM) you the one (F).
50	C:	Hum, hum.
51	S:	Or, it is also good if you would like to pay (H) monthly until the day of maturity (F).
52	C:	Hum.
53	S:	However, if you say (H) that you need a sewing machine, you can take (H) it (F). As you know (H), Okusan [meaning housewife], electric products are cheaper (F).
54	C:	However, we don't use it at our house. It's enough if we have one.
55	S:	How about one when your daughter (H) marries (H) (F)?
56	C:	We'll think of it, that time. She is still a student.
57	S:	Is she in junior high or senior high (F)?
58	C:	In college.
59	S:	Oh, in college. Well now.
60	C:	Anyway, she is not lady-like. Our daughter is (2).
61	S:	Oh, what are you talking (H) about (F)?
62	C:	Yes, it is true. She is not the type of a girl who needs a sewing machine (F).
63	S:	If she looks like you (H), she is (2).
64	C:	Oh no. She says that she wants to find some occupation. Besides, she is in the midst of studying (F).
65	S:	Is she in the English department (F)?
66	C:	No.
67	S:	Home economics?
68	C:	No, no. She is not the type of person who studies those subjects.
69	S:	I don't believe so. Hum. Hum.
70	C:	I'm telling you that she is not the type of a lady who uses sewing machine at home (F). We already have one. Therefore (3).
71	S:	Hum, hum.
72	C:	One machine can do anyway (2).

73 S: If you pay 3,000 yen, it will take a little longer three years (F).
74 C: Yeah.
75 S: Maybe, it is the time for your daughter (H) to marry and it will be good for that preparation (F).
76 C: When she marries, let's buy it that time. Nobody knows when she will marry. We don't even know if she will marry (F).
77 S: What are you talking about? You shouldn't worry about that, *Okusan* (F).
78 C: (laughter) Hum.
79 S: In ordinary cases, this (3). You know in the television (1). Electronic one.
80 C: Yeah, yeah.
81 S: That one (2). If you pay a deposit, it costs 150,000 yen (F).
82 C: Hum, hum.
83 S: Well, if you pay monthly, it costs a little more than 140,000 yen (F). Therefore, it is good if the things become cheaper from now (F), but if you think of everything going up, it is better for you to pay (H) 3,000 yen monthly (F) and to be ready to buy it. A little bit more than three years ahead (1) for your daughter (F). It is cheaper (H) (2). The balance of raising things and the 450 yen's interest you will receive 15 percent (2). Usually even in the bank, you cannot receive that interest. I am telling you that you will receive 450 yen (F), 450 yen a month means 4,500 yen for 10 months. If you deposit (H) 30,000 yen, you will receive 4,500 yen (F).
84 C: Hum, hum.
85 S: Then.
86 C: I don't think so.
87 S: Yes, our company does guarantee it (F).
88 C: If you are doing so, your company (H) will be ruined.
89 S: Oh, no. The famous J company will never be ruined (F). This is (2). Well, it is true (F). If you pay monthly (2). This is, as you know, there is one called *Portable*. This is it (F). This costs 140,000 (F). *The eye of the electron*. This is it, *Okusan* (H). This is it (F). This is (F). This new one is called *Oilless* which means we don't need oiling (F). You know that electric fan, Oilless electric fan.
90 C: Yea.
91 S: That is the same. Well, I told you *cam*. This is it (F). (S shows the picture of *cam*.) This already contains an electron. If we want to fix the television channel (F), it lights up (F). And the place that is lighted means ready to function (F). This is it (F). If you turn this, for example (1). Is yours (H) *Free Arm* (F)?

92 C: I don't remember.   Because she bought it.   I don't know.

93 S: Is that so.   This is good even for trousers.   If you push one bottom by the auxiliary tape, it is inserted inside (F).   This is shaped like this and called *Portable* (F).   This is the one being advertised now on the television (F).   An electronic one available for both thick and thin clothes (F).

94 C: Hum, hum.

95 S: It is really called the combination of electron (F), therefore, in case of the thread, you can manage within a moment (F).   The rear will drop if you simply push the red button (F).   Very simple, very simple, because it is working by electron.   There is (H) an electronic lighter, isn't there (F)?   That's it (F).   This, this, this is it (F).   If you pay monthly it costs 158,000 yen (F).   One hundred forty-two thousand yen means a balance of 450 yen times 10, which amounts to 45,000 yen (F).   Therefore, suppose you want to contract (H) now, if you (H) do as you know, you will get (H) the merchandise under this price (H) (F).   It will be done definitely (F).   (S shows a written guarantee to C.) So, there is no mistake about this, *Okusan* (H) (F).

96 C: Hum, hum.

97 S: Therefore, the balance (2).   It is this.   In case of cash, one//hundred fifty thousand...

98 C: But* nobody knows about three years later, right? Like inflation and it will change the value of money. If the value of money will change.

99 S: Oh, no.   Even if it happens, G company will unmistakably deliver (H) the merchandise under this price (H) (F).   If something happens in violation of this promise it is to commit a fraud (F).   Also, securities will cause problem.

100 C: Hum, hum.

101 S: I mean that once we receive a contract from you, we secure the merchandise for you (F).   There is (H) no mistake about this (F).   For example, the Association consumers would complain (F).   Therefore, *Okusan* (H) there is no mistake about this (F).

102 C: Is that so?   Is this called special fishhook?

103 S: Yes, you can do anything with this (F).   With only one button.

104 C: Hum, hum.

105 S: You can do anything (F).   I made this button hole within 30 seconds (F).   I did it within 30 seconds. With this sewing machine we can sew this very thin cloth (F).   If you use old one, you will find that the thread will be tangled.   The thread.

106 C: Well, I will consider it, again.

107 S: Is that so (F)?

108 C: Hum, besides, we have one already.

109 S: Well, I thought it good (H) for your daughter. (H) (F). At any rate, it is more beneficial (H). This balance (2). This is much more beneficial than this (H). Fifteen percent interest is true (F). The company guarantees it (F). Therefore, for 10 months, 4,500 yen out of 30,000 (F), 30,000 yen (2). This is 4,500 yen, isn't it (F)? In a year, it amounts 36,000 yen. Therefore, we add 900 yen and we have 5,400 yen. You will get 54,000 yen as an interest (F). And this interest add here. As a result, you have the balance of this amount (F). Consequently, it will be more beneficial (H) for you *Okusan* (H), to buy (H) it by monthly installment than by cash (F).

110 C: Hum, hum.

111 S: Yes, you can buy this by monthly installment for this price (H) (F). Therefore (2) I understand that your daughter (H) is in school (F), so 3,000 yen (1).

112 C: After all, you get money in advance and so you will do the interest.

113 S: Yes, ha ha ha (laughter). However, even if you deposit money in the bank, there is (F) nowhere that you will get 15% interest. I mean 450 yen for 3,000 yen (F). There is no mistake about this (F). J company guarantees it (F). Therefore, everybody says (H) that this sewing machine is easy for both thin and thick ones and also handy to carry (F). They say portable is more convenient so they choose (H) this kind.

114 C: I agree. Yes. But I'm not sure for our case.

115 S: Three years later. It's for your daughter's (H) marriage (H). Three thousand yen monthly means 100 yen for a day (F). It's more beneficial (H) to spend 3,000 yen (F).

116 C: Frankly speaking, we don't know what will happen in the future. It's not even sure if she will stay in Japan (F).

117 S: Hum, hum.

118 C: So, well, we can't prepare anything for the future (F). Truly. We should do it according to the situation when the future arrives.

119 S: Think that you save (H) money in the bank and withdraw (H) it later (2). Only one (H) daughter (H) (F)?

120 C: Two, but.

121 S: Well, then, the younger one (H) will be also able to use it (F). Is she (H) in high school (F)?

122 C: But, we already have one.

123 S: Hum, hum. One machine certainly (1). You cannot sew (H) with this kind (F). The ladies especially who have (H) interest (2). These kinds (2). I sewed this. It's very simple, it moves automatically (F). We can

adjust slow or fast. If you do it fast, it goes fast (F). If you want to do it slowly, it goes slowly (F).

124 C: Is that so? Well, I will consider it. So suddenly I (2).

125 S: Yes.

126 C: I can't decide so suddenly (2).

127 S: Well, *Okusan* (H) then, shall I leave (HM) catalog (F)?

128 C: Well, OK. We have visits several times from your companies.

129 S: Well, this is. Write here and if you mail (H) this (F) (3) the catalog (2).

130 C: All right.

131 S: If you write (H) your name (H) and address (H) here and mark (H) this, we would like to send (HM) it (F).

132 C: I understand.

133 S: You don't need any stamps (F).

134 C: Yes, sir (F).

135 S: Well, today at 3:00 on television on Channel 8 you know (H) that?

136 C: I don't watch television so often.

137 S: Is that so? On Monday, from 9, at Momotarō ( ). This is also sponsored by J. Well, even a child (H) can carry this. Besides, it's not so heavy. It is *Free Arm* isn't it (F). At first, there are many housewives (H) who admit (H) that it is very convenient (F) because we don't need to change color. Well, I'm sorry to say but you can write (H) down and (2) (refers to paper 1 gives).

138 C: Yes.

139 S: Well, please mail (H) it, when you want (F).

140 C: Yes, all right.

141 S: Well, please give (H) our best regards to your daughters (H) (F).

142 C: Yes, I will.

143 S: Excuse me (HM), while you are so busy (H).

144 C: Yes.

145 S: Well, good-bye (F).

146 C: Yes, good-bye.

3.5.5 Analysis of speech acts. (1) In the foregoing conversation, the distribution of moves is as follows: 93 moves by S and 79 moves by C.

(2) S calls C *Okusan* 'housewife (honorific form)', but C does not use any address forms to S. However, when C refers to S's company and S's business, she uses a category-term, the name of the company and honorific suffix *san*. (This usage is explained more in detail in Chapters 5 and 6.)

(3) When S identifies himself, he gives only the name of the company to which he belongs. Therefore, neither of the participants is aware of the other's personal name during the course of

the conversation.

(4) Honorific usages and humble forms are frequently used by S, but neither of these forms is used by C.

(5) S and C use different vocabulary to signify C's daughter since S uses a relevant honorific form and C uses a plain form: S uses *ojōsan* 'daughter (honorific form)' and C uses *musume* 'daughter (nonhonorific form)'.

(6) Formal speech patterns are frequently used by S but since S's and C's social status is similar (that is, middle class), formal speech patterns in S's utterances are characterized as the informal style by the frequent use of the postpositional particle *ne*. S uses it 75 times and C uses it 23 times. (Levels of formality in Japanese are discussed in detail in a later chapter.) The distribution of the use of *ne* according to its function is shown in Table 3.5.

Table 3.5 Use of postpositional particle *ne*.

		S	C
Function 1:	Expresses a feeling of indirect judgment	18	9
Function 2:	Renders a feeling of indirect insistence	20	1
Function 3:	Asks agreement and answers to response	1	0
Function 4:	Asks question indirectly	2	0
Function 5:	Emphasizes the expression	18	0
Function 6:	Serves as a linking marker with the next topic	16	7

The other postpositional particle used by S and C is *yo*. This particle has two functions: (1) to insist and draw a conclusion, and (2) to attract attention. The distribution of the use of *yo* according to its function is given in Table 3.6.

Table 3.6 Use of postpositional particle *yo*.

	Number of times used:	
	By S:	By C:
Function 1:	15	14
Function 2:	6	1

(7) From the conversational exchange emerge distinct patterns typical of male and female speech. These patterns are characterized by the different use of the postpositional particle. For example, C answers as a response to a question by S, *J ja nakatta kashira* 'J brand, I wonder'. The postpositional particle *kashira* is traditionally reserved for female speakers.

(8) As a greeting formula, S uses an expression of apology, *Excuse me,* and this expression later reoccurs as an expression of gratitude: *Excuse me, while you are so busy.* Another characteristic of S's use of speech in regard to greeting is that he requests C to extend his regards to the daughters even though they have never met.

(9) S shows gratitude by thanking C, when he hears that C already owns a sewing machine of his brand.

(10) A persuasive quality is very noticeable in S's speech throughout the encounter. Basically, he uses two positive approaches in his attempt to convince C of the desirability of purchasing his product: (1) he points out benefits of the machine; (2) he explains why and how C can buy the machine more cheaply.

Occasionally, he tries to persuade C by including both of these benefits in a single utterance. The following list indicates S's repetitious use of the two positive points just mentioned.

U 21:	point 1	U 103:	1
U 43:	2	U 105:	1
U 79:	1	U 109:	2
U 81:	2	U 111:	2
U 83:	2	U 113:	2 and 1
U 89:	2 and 1	U 115:	2
U 91:	1	U 119:	2
U 93:	1	U 123:	1
U 95:	1 and 2	U 137:	1
U 101:	1		

(11) S's explicit request that C purchase his product is limited to a single expression, *For your daughter's marriage, how about one?* (U 39). This usage contrasts with the great variety of direct request forms employed by the American cosmetic salesman in Section 3.4.

(12) When C tries to decline purchase of S's merchandise, she refuses indirectly:

U 22: We already have one now. It's enough for my house.
U 34: Therefore, there is no way.
U 54: However, we don't use it at our house. It's enough if we have one.
U 72: One machine can do anyway.
U 106: Well, I will consider it, again.
U 108: Besides, we have one already.
U 114: I agree...but I'm not sure for our case.
U 118: So, well, we can't prepare anything for the future, truly...
U 122: But, we already have one.
U 124: Is that so? Well, I will consider it...
U 126: I can't decide so suddenly...

(13) S's speech pattern is also characterized by the fact that some utterances can be further classified into smaller units, that is, moves. Some examples are given here.

U 39: (1) suggestion of purchase
(2) explanation
U 89: (1) response to C
(2) explanation of how to buy more cheaply
(3) emphasis on benefit of the machine
U 95: (1) explanation about benefit of the machine
(2) emphasis on how to buy more cheaply
(3) explanation of why he says there are no mistakes
U 119: (1) comparison with analogous situation
(2) asking questions

3.5.6 Narrative structure. The conversation began with S's greeting and identification. Then S initiated his conversation by probing whether C knew about the special sewing machine advertised on television. All through the business talk, S repeatedly explained the benefits and economy of his product and tried to convince C about these features. He insistently proposes a connection between C's purchase of his product and the advantage to C's daughters. With C's utterance, *I can't decide so suddenly*, which implied her desire to terminate the business talk with S, the conversation entered a new stage. S stopped trying to persuade C and tried instead to leave some

Figure 3.4 Structure of a door-to-door sales transaction in the Japanese speech community.

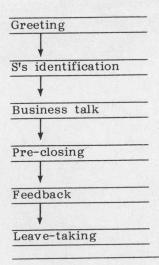

Greeting

S's identification

Business talk

Pre-closing

Feedback

Leave-taking

literature so that C could continue the contact with the J sewing machine company whenever she wished. However, to provide a feedback of his sales talk, S again mentioned his company's television commercial and emphasized the benefits of his product one final time. Then, S showed gratitude for his visit by way of apology, as is typical of Japanese speech pattern, and the conversation finally concluded. The general organization of the whole conversation is shown in Figure 3.4.

CHAPTER FOUR

STRUCTURAL ANALYSIS OF SALES TRANSACTIONS

4.0   Introduction.   In Chapter 3, four specific sales events were provided and discussed. Chapter 4 aims at formulating a more general overview by considering many more examples of each type of speech pattern and by analyzing the information in greater detail.

The three general categories to be considered in this chapter are: (1) interpretation of data according to similarities and differences within the two speech communities; (2) investigation of overall patterns of sales transactions; and (3) identification and description of sociocultural variables which affect speech patterns. Throughout these stages, both the American and Japanese speech communities are considered.

4.1   Comparative analysis on the basis of sales types.   In order to investigate the structure of the various types of sales transactions in the American and Japanese speech communities, the pattern of each type is explained according to the following outline: (1) institutional sales, (2) door-to-door sales, (3) department store sales, (4) sales in private stores, (5) sales in markets, (6) sales by street hawkers, (7) sales by public address in markets, (8) sales by public address in department stores, and (9) sales by public address on the train. Types (8) and (9) are not investigated in the American speech community because of lack of data. These types of sales transactions do not seem to be widespread within American culture.

4.1.1   Institutional sales.   Data of this type collected in the Japanese speech community are all related to drug salesmen who visit hospitals regularly. The common feature of this type of salespeople is that they dress neatly in a suit and with highly polished shoes. Their courteous attitude toward the doctors and pharmacists is reflected by their frequent bows, and their behavior has an almost ritualistic quality. Their speech pattern is characterized by frequent use of honorific forms and humble forms in formal style.

61

Salesmen's talk of this type usually begins with a greeting. In some cases, the salesmen proceed directly to their business talk. In other cases, before discussing the major topic of business, the salesmen bring up some relevant topics, e.g. comment about academic meetings, etc. In still other cases, the statement of the visit's purpose immediately follows greetings, before the actual business transaction is initiated. In the next step, 'approach', salesmen provide introductory remarks about their product, e.g. explain a new medicine, emphasizing merits and effects. If the purpose of the visit is only to consult with the doctors about the effectiveness of the medicine and not to obtain an actual sale, the salesmen take leave, expressing thanks for the visit. In other cases, right after the business transaction is terminated and before leave-taking, either the customer or salesman introduces new topics for continued discussion. For the Japanese speech community, the general pattern of this type of salesmen's talk is shown in Figure 4.1.

Figure 4.1 Institutional sales in the Japanese speech community.

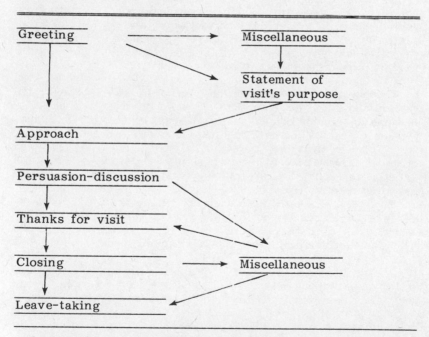

Data on this type of institutional sale collected in the American speech community can be divided into three categories: (1) drug salesmen who visit hospitals regularly, (2) salesmen of office and surgical supplies who visit hospitals, and (3) food salespeople who visit various institutions. The common feature of the salespeople of all three categories is similar to that of salespeople in the Japanese speech community. Salesmen are all neatly dressed in suit and tie, and saleswomen wear a one-piece dress or a suit. Their speech pattern, however, is informal and rather casual. Both salespeople and customers seem to enjoy friendly talk and joking, with functional gestures and occasional laughter.

The conversation begins with a greeting. Sometimes before the business talk, casual conversation, e.g. about daily life or social contemporary issues, follows the greeting. One of the characteristics of this type of sales transaction in the American speech community is that this kind of miscellaneous topic can be observed in any stage of the conversation. For example, in the middle of the business talk, during the short period when the buyers are checking the invoice, salesmen make friendly inquiries about such things as weekend activities. After the closing of the business talk and before leave-taking, this kind of conversation is also inserted. It is true that this flexibility is noticeable in the American speech community, but compared with the 'chat' in the Japanese speech community, the time span is much shorter. Since salespeople and customers are exchanging conversation on an equal basis, a more enjoyable and carefree atmosphere prevails than in the Japanese speech community. The equality of salesperson and customer is evidenced by the same level of informality used by both, and by the more balanced quantity of speech from each during the interaction. The general pattern of institutional sales transactions in the American speech community is shown in Figure 4.2.

Figure 4.2 Institutional sales in the American speech community.

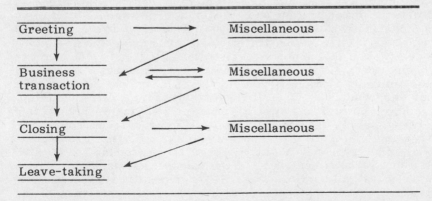

4.1.2 Door-to-door sales. A total of 23 sales events of this type were collected in the Japanese speech community (see list in Table 3.1). The commodities or services sold by the different salespeople fall into six categories: (1) advertising, (2) office and school supplies, (3) insurance, (4) cars, (5) electric appliances, and (6) stocks. Although the procedure of each sales transaction in the data is more or less the same, regardless of the commodities or services, there is great variation in the number of turn-takings between salespeople and customers. The shortest one is composed of only three turns by the salesman and the customer, respectively. At the other end of the spectrum, the longest recording transcript of this type shows that the salesperson and the customer speak 126 times each. During these exchanges, the salesperson plays a predominant role in two ways: (1) his utterance is always longer and (2) one utterance, in some cases, can be further classified into smaller units. The two major factors of his long talk are (1) repetitious explanation of the advantages of his own product and (2) introduction, during or after the stage of persuasion, of some topics not directly related to the business transaction but still relevant. In spite of the differences in length of the various examples within this category, however, the same internal structure of sales transactions can be observed, as indicated in Figure 4.3.

Only one example of this type was collected from the American speech community, and this example may not be considered typical because it involved multiple customers. The data show that the conversation begins with a greeting by a saleswoman who visits door-to-door selling a certain brand of cosmetics. She visits individual homes upon request from her friends and acquaintances of her family. Therefore, by contrast with the usage of the Japanese speech community, it is unlikely that this type salesperson will identify herself after the initial greeting. Instead, she fosters the informal atmosphere of the situation by a friendly account of her activities earlier in the day. The second stage of this type of interaction which is apparent in the data is demonstration and explanation of the products. In this specific sales transaction, miscellaneous matter occurs in this stage. After demonstrating and explaining the products, the saleswoman distributes a registration card and order form to each customer. Here again, as in the second stage, the saleswoman and customers actively engage in questions and answers about the product. Then, before leave-taking, the hostess of the house who invited the saleswoman as well as the prospective customers serves refreshments and all enjoy a social hour. As is true in the Japanese speech community, analysis of data evidences high frequency of turn-takings and abundant use of complex and compound sentences in the salesperson's speech. These are elements which can rarely be observed in the customers' utterances in either speech community. The interaction of the salesperson and customers is explained in Figure 4.4.

4.1.3   Department store sales.   In Japan, there is throughout these transactions a similarity in the appearance of the department store salespersons, all of whom wear uniforms

Figure 4.3 Door-to-door sales transactions in the Japanese speech community.

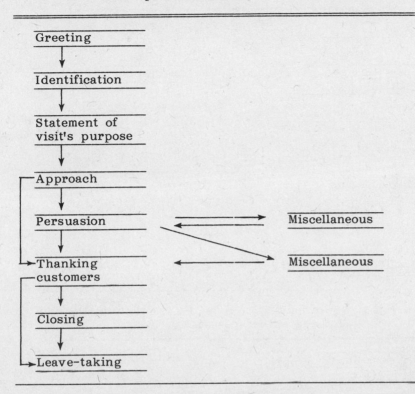

according to Japanese custom. There is also great similarity in their speech patterns because they all, regardless of sex, frequently use polite forms and formal styles. Figure 4.5 presents the important stages of department store sales in Japan. As Figure 4.5 indicates, the first and second stages are optional. If the salesperson is relatively sure, through observation, about the customer's wishes, he initiates conversation simply by inquiring about the customer's specific interest or by explaining about the merchandise. Thus, in this situation, the third stage, 'approach', plays the role of initiator of the conversation.

In the American speech community, the general pattern of this type is more or less the same as that of the Japanese speech community. One difference is that salespeople in the American speech community do not usually wear uniforms. Instead, some salespeople wear a name tag to identify themselves. Another difference is that their speech pattern is not characterized by the conventionalized use of polite expressions as is the case with the Japanese speech community. This means that in the American speech community there is not a definite prescribed

Figure 4.4 Door-to-door sales transactions in the American speech community.

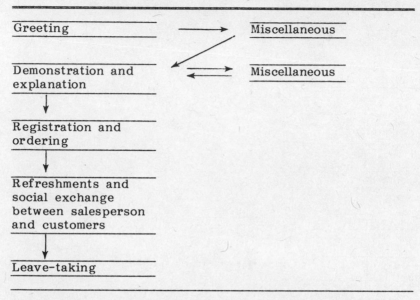

Figure 4.5 Department store sales transactions in the Japanese speech community.

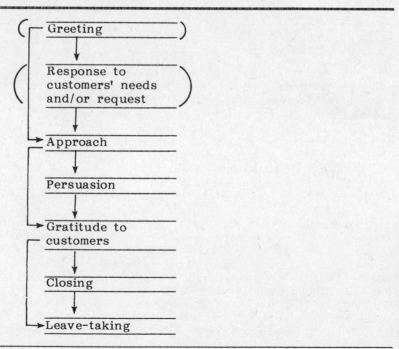

speech level; the choice depends rather on the salesperson's will and intentions. The general pattern of sales transactions in the American speech community is shown in Figure 4.6.

Figure 4.6 Department store sales transactions in the American speech community.

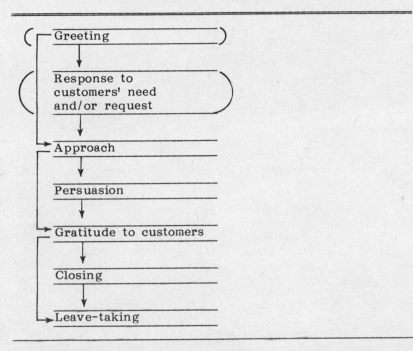

4.1.4   Sales in private stores. A total of 154 examples were collected in the Japanese speech community concerning this type. Of these, 142 events were observed and recorded on different dates and at different times in the same drug store, which sells medicine, cosmetics, and general household supplies. The store is located in the Tokyo suburbs and most of the customers are known to the salesperson, who is the pharmacist's wife. This adds another feature to this type of speech pattern in cases where both salesperson and customer share the same role, that of housewife. It is apparent that the data often contain topics that are not related to business talk, and in some cases the salesperson and the customer spend more time talking and exchanging opinions about subjects other than business. Out of a total of 142 events, 45 are of this type, that is, the salesperson welcomes a customer who is, like herself, a housewife. In a total of 45 events, 36 (80%) show that in this situation the participants spend more time chatting and sharing their opinions about nonbusiness topics. The types of subjects the salesperson discusses with the customer are as follows.

Subject: *Frequency:*

child care   7
weather   5
husband's job   4
children's school education   5
vacation plans   4
menu for meals   3
visit to parents   3
child delivery   2
purchase of car   1
purchase of house   1
family birthday   1

                            Total: 36

Another characteristic of this type of sale is the variety of
speech repertoires used by both salesperson and customers. In
some cases, (1) only the salesperson uses polite forms with
honorifics; in other cases, (2) only customers use polite forms;
and in still other cases, (3) both salesperson and customers use
polite forms. In these instances, the use of polite forms with
honorifics and of humble forms is not consistent on the part of
the salesperson, a fact which deviates from usual usage within
the Japanese speech community. The variety of speech repertoires in this specific situation is due to role ambiguity. In
the ordinary situation, the Japanese customer expects the salesperson to employ honorifics and humble forms. In the foregoing
situations, however, the role expectation is ambiguous because
of factors like the following: (1) both salesperson and customer share the common role of housewife, live in the same neighborhood, and have social contacts beyond the business transaction here recorded; and (2) in some cases, children of both
parties attend the same school and the children of the salesperson, being older, take care of the smaller children of the
customer. Therefore, the customer also feels obliged to express
deference and appreciation through use of honorifics and humble
forms to the salesperson.

The general pattern of sales transactions in Japanese private
stores is given in Figure 4.7. As discussed earlier, the
miscellaneous category has an important function in the sales
transaction when both the salesperson and customer are housewives. For this reason, this category has been included in
Figure 4.7, which diagrams the principal parts of the face-to-
face interaction in the Japanese speech community.

Based on the data collected within the American speech community, it is obvious that the salesperson's attitude is more
business-like than in the Japanese speech community. The salesperson seldom comments on personal matters or on topics other
than the merchandise he is dealing with. This may be because
the salesperson does not know any of the customers and believes
that efficiency is the most important quality in a good sales-

Figure 4.7 Sales transactions in private stores in the Japanese speech community.

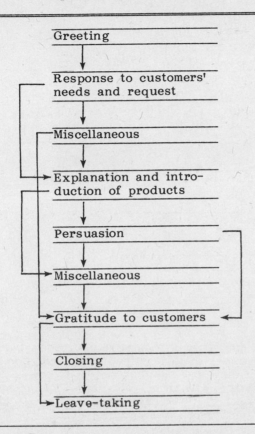

person. Figure 4.8 shows the procedures that can be observed in the interaction between salesperson and customers in the American speech community.

In the simplest example, the interaction between salesperson and customer occurs only in the third stage, according to Figure 4.8. Some American salespeople terminate the contact without formal stages of closing or leave-taking.

4.1.5 Sales in markets. In the Japanese speech community, the data indicate that market sales are always initiated by the hawking of a salesperson whose voice ranges from a low to high intonation. This is one of the strategies this type of salesperson employs to attract customers' attention and to get them to pause before the merchandise he is selling. Another chracteristic which this type of sale shares with door-to-door sales is that the salesperson frequently repeats the same utter-

Figure 4.8   Sales transactions in private stores in the
American speech community.

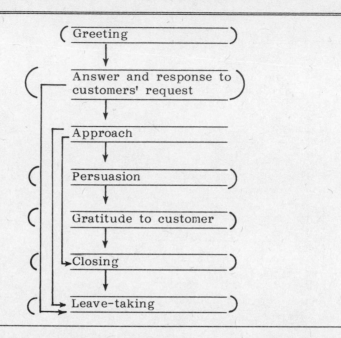

ance over and over again. However, the salesperson's utterance
at the market is shorter, nonnarrative, and contains many
imperatives. Another interesting fact is that this kind of
speech pattern correlates with the salesperson's appearance:
when he is casually dressed, this speech pattern is also casual,
with no polite forms, no honorifics, and no formal style. The
salesperson is usually a middle-aged male. His customary attire
includes a headband, a casual shirt or at times no shirt, only a
belly band and short pants. His speech is often marked as male
speech by the frequent use of a few definite postpositional
particles which are used only by men. Figure 4.9 shows the
general pattern of this type of sale.

Sales in flea markets in the American speech community reveal
the following differences from market sales in the Japanese
speech community: (1) speech patterns contain no indication of
the gender of the salesperson, (2) address forms are different.
In the Japanese speech community, the salesperson addresses
housewives as *okusan* 'one who is at home (plus the honorific
suffix -*san*)'. In the American speech community, salespersons do not address customers on the basis of their status in
the family. (This aspect is explained in greater detail later
in this chapter.) Figure 4.10 shows the general pattern of flea
market sales in the American speech community.

Figure 4.9 Sales transactions in markets in the Japanese speech community.

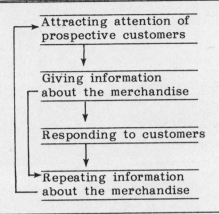

Figure 4.10 Sales transactions in flea markets in the American speech community.

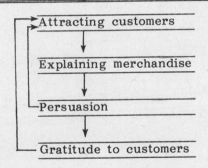

4.1.6 Sales by street hawkers. Data on this type of sales transaction in the Japanese speech community show marked similarities with sales transactions in markets. First of all, the salesperson in both sales transactions wears a casual shirt with a towel around his head and speaks very informally, using plain forms. Second, the use of imperatives is frequently observed in face-to-face interaction with customers. Third, the postpositional particles used by the salesperson indicate the salesperson's sex. However, sales by street hawkers are charac-terized by the fact that the salesperson attempts to establish a more friendly atmosphere with the customers. This may be because their physical distance is closer than is the case in the market, where sometimes the salesperson calls out through a microphone. One of the street hawkers selling flowers addresses the prospective customer, whose age would be similar to his own mother's, as *okasan* 'mother', and explains the story of his own mother's death. The customer, in turn, comments on the story and encourages the salesperson in the course of conversational interaction. It is most likely that the salesperson did not know anything about the customer's background. Neither did the customer know about the sad history of the salesperson, but through the informal conversation between them, they have a real human encounter, at least a glimpse of one. The general pattern of this type of sale is similar to that of sales in the markets, as shown in figure 4.11.

Figure 4.11 Street hawkers' sales transactions in the Japanese speech community.

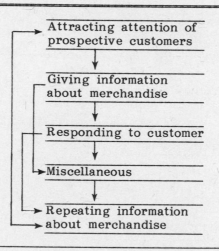

Attracting attention of prospective customers

Giving information about merchandise

Responding to customer

Miscellaneous

Repeating information about merchandise

Data on sales by street hawkers in the American speech community indicate that the interaction between a salesperson and a customer is shorter and more impersonal than in the Japanese speech community. This difference can also be observed between the two speech communities with regard to sales transactions in private stores. In the American speech community, the street hawker seems to behave like a businessman. He does not try to create a personal relationship with a customer but tries, instead, to keep their relationship on a business level only. The street hawker's speech pattern is characterized by the sentence without any subject, e.g. *Want a bag?* or by the repetitious use of a simple pattern, e.g. *Incense stick one dollar, incense 50 sticks one dollar, 50 sticks one dollar...* Another difference from this type of sale in the Japanese speech community is that there is no marker to indicate the gender of the salesperson. The general pattern of this type of interaction is shown in Figure 4.12.

Figure 4.12 Street hawker's sales transactions in the American speech community.

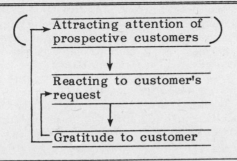

4.1.7 Sales by public address in markets. With regard to sales by public address, the differences between the American and Japanese speech communities can be summarized as follows: (1) in the Japanese speech community, there is frequent use throughout the message of honorifics and polite forms in formal-formal styles, while in the American speech community these features cannot be observed; (2) in the Japanese speech community, the same message, containing the same sentence structure, is used repeatedly over and over again, while in the American speech community this characteristic, though sometimes noted, is not standard; (3) naturally, because of the aforementioned characteristics, the public address performance in the Japanese speech community is much longer and more complete; (4) the tone and voice of the Japanese salesperson indicate emotional involvement, while this feature is rarely observed within the American speech community.

4.1.8 Sales by public address in department stores. The Japanese data indicate very frequent use of honorific, polite forms in formal-formal styles. No address forms are used and in many cases the sentences have no real grammatical subjects or agents. The message is addressed in general to any clients in the department store and the customers are completely at ease with the message, which lacks the basic relationship of 'who' is going to inform 'whom' regarding sales possibilities. This may be because an underlying belief exists among the Japanese that the expression without agent, either first person or second person, in formal-formal style conveys the message most politely. Another characteristic of this type of public address is the use of *Kango* forms in formal-formal styles. *Kango* forms were originally borrowed from the Chinese linguistic system but are now included as expressions in the Japanese linguistic system together with *Yamato Kotoba* 'forms which are Japanese in origin'. According to an investigation by the National Language Research Institute (Kokuritsu Kokugo Kenyūsho), Japanese people believe that the use of *Kango* indicates a higher level of courtesy than *Yamato Kotoba* (Kokuritsu Kokugo Kenkyūsho 1957:376).

4.1.9 Sales by public address on the train. The announcement is characterized by frequent use of honorific polite forms in the formal-formal style. Address forms are not used but when the message refers to the passengers in general, a vocabulary *minasama* 'you (plural)(honorific)' is used. The data exhibit great similarities with those of the foregoing categories of public address in markets and in department stores: all employ the frequent use of honorifics, polite forms, and the occasional use of humble forms in formal-formal style. Similarly, on the train, the address is initiated by a message which lacks an agent, as is also the case with the public message in the department store.

4.2 Overall pattern of sales transactions. With regard to the general pattern of sales transactions, there are pronounced similarities in the procedures of each of the two speech communities. The three obvious stages of these procedures are the opening, the middle, and the closing. Each of these has standard subcomponents. The opening ordinarily consists of greeting and identification. The parties to the transaction greet each other and if the salesman is unknown to the customers, he provides identification. The middle stage, the business transaction, usually consists of approach and negotiation. In the approach stage, the customer, or more commonly, the salesperson, initiates the transaction. The negotiation includes any discussion, explanation, bargaining, and either the acceptance or refusal of the merchandise or service in question. Finally, the closing segment contains the pre-closing and the leave-taking. In pre-closing, either customer, salesperson, or both manifest their desire to terminate the transaction. Leave-taking, the ending sequence, consists of the expression of gratitude, courtesy, and the exchange of certain terminal formulas.

These procedures are outlined in Figure 4.13 and are commented upon in greater detail in the continuing narrative.

Figure 4.13 Overall pattern of sales transactions.

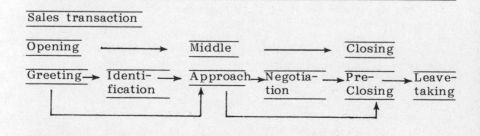

4.2.1 Opening.

4.2.1.1 Greeting. The simplest pattern of greeting observed in both speech communities is an adjacency pair of greeting-greeting between customer and salesperson. Two patterns can be seen. In the first, the salesperson (S) initiates and the customer (C) answers.

(1) S: Good morning. (F)
    C: Good morning. (D) (Japanese speech community (JC), private store)
(2) S: Hi!
    C: Hi! (American speech community (AC), department store)

In the second case, C initiates.

(3) C: Good morning.
    S: Good morning, sir. (AC institutional)
(4) C: How are you feeling, all right?
    S: Yeah, I'm in pretty good shape. (AC institutional)

In the foregoing examples, S and C know each other and S does not feel it necessary to identify himself. However, when C does not know S or when S is not sure that C knows him, C identifies himself right after the initial greeting.

(5) S: How're you doing? I'm with U (a company's name).
    C: OK. (AC institutional)
(6) S: Good afternoon. (F) I am (HM) from M (company's name).
    C: Yes. (JC institutional)

Examples (5) and (6) were collected in the conversation between a customer and a salesman who visits institutions like hospitals, schools, and companies. When the salespeople do not know the customers and still want to direct a greeting to them, the adjacency pair of greeting is not employed because there is no immediate response from the customer.

(7) S: Hi, ladies! (AC flea market)
(8) S: Hey ladies, welcome! (JC market)
(9) S: Welcome, mother! (JC market)
(10) S: Come in, folks! (AC flea market)

Sometimes a customer initiates the conversation with a greeting and immediately adds a statement about what he wants. Consequently, in this case, since the salesman replies not to the customer's greeting but to his request, the adjacency pair formula of greeting is again not employed.

(11) C: Hello!   Could you please tell me if you handle
          the things that convert scores into marks?
      S: Uh, yeah. (AC private store)
(12) C: Good afternoon. (F) Please give me a medicine for
          a cold.
      S: Sure. (F) (JC private store)

In still other cases, immediately after the exchange of greetings, topics like the weather or weekend activities are brought
up when S and C know each other. This conversational sequence
serves as a bridge between the first and second stages of the
sales transaction, that is, between the initial exchange of
greeting and the approach.

(13) S: Good morning. (H) (F)
      C: Good morning. (H) (F)
      S: Isn't it hot? (H) (F)
      C: Yes, indeed. I hate even to cook (H) on such a
          terrible day.
      S: I don't blame you. (F) (JC private store)
(14) S: Good morning, Mr. O. How are you, sir?
      C: How are you doing, R (first name)?
      S: Oh, pretty good. Have a good weekend, J?
      C: Well, let's see (2).   I didn't do anything.
          Didn't do anything. Didn't do anything.
      S: Well, I didn't do much myself.   (AC institution-
          al)

Immediately after these exchanges, the parties initiate the
business transaction.
   In addition to the foregoing greeting patterns which are employed in both speech communities, in the Japanese speech community the following ritualistic formula is often used between
door-to-door salesmen and customers.

(15) S: Excuse me. (HM) I am (HM) from J company (F).
          Is (H) the President (H) (of the company) at home
          (H)(F)?
      C: No, he isn't. (JC door-to-door)

The first greeting ritual *Excuse me* implies the speaker's
own attitude toward the customer.   Even if the expression is
ritualistic formula here, the original meaning came from the
humility of the salesperson, who considered himself a distur-
bance to the customer. This formula is a self-contained expression which does not require response or answer from the addressee. Another common speech pattern of greeting among Japanese salespersons who visit institutions or private houses is
that they express gratitude for the support they have received
from customers in the form of greeting.

(16) C: Please come in.
      S: Thank you so much for the patronage (H) (F). I
          am (HM) from M (company's name) and my name is (HM)
          T. (F) (JC door-to-door)

The formula in example (16) can be well understood when we
realize that an important aspect of greeting in Japanese society
is to express gratitude for what the addressee did when he saw
the speaker last. This is true even if there has been a long
lapse of time since they saw each other, e.g. *Thank you for
the previous occasion (F)* or *Thank you for the excellent
dinner the other day (F)*. These formulas serve as greetings
and create a good atmosphere in which to continue the conversation if the speakers have some topics in mind. Besides, this
feeling of gratitude can be extended to benefits which the
addresser may receive from the addressee. For example, when a
mother meets the future homeroom teacher of her daughter, she
greets the teacher as shown in example (17), accompanying the
conversation with a deep bow and using honorifics.

(17) Mother: I am the mother of A (F). (You) will be
                caring (H) for her for which I am most grate-
                ful (F).
      Teacher: All right.

Similarly, it is observed that the institutional salesman uses
this formula when he has an initial encounter with the customer,
as in (18).

(18) S: Pardon (HM) me. I see (HM) (you) for the first
          time (F). Thank you for the patronage (H) (F). I
          am (HM) from K company.
      C: K company? (JC institutional)

This expression of gratitude is also often used by the salesperson in the department store or private store in a formula like
Welcome (F), thank you for the patronage (H) (F).

These characteristics of Japanese greeting provide an interesting contrast with the typical greeting in the American speech
community, where the initial exchange of greeting between the
salesman and the customer is likely to be more friendly, personal, and reciprocal. For example, the institutional salesman in
the American speech community begins his greeting as in example
(19).

(19) S: Hi-ya Paul.
      C: Hello, how's doing? (AC institutional)

The pattern in (19) is still appropriate even if S's and C's
roles are reversed. Thus, C begins the conversation in (20).

(20)   C: Hi-ya Paul.
       S: Hello, how's doing?

This reciprocal pattern shows that the greeting exchange of American salespeople and their customers is egalitarian and friendly, contrary to the Japanese way of greeting, which is nonreciprocal.

4.2.1.2 Identification. The way in which the salesperson identifies himself to the customer is also worth observing. Data collected in both speech communities demonstrate that 20 out of 39 Japanese salesmen who visited institutions or private houses identified themselves to the customers. Sixteen institutional salesmen included in this group had no need for spoken identification as they had already given a business card to the prospective customers. All of the salesmen who gave spoken identification indicated, first of all, the name of the company to which they belonged. Besides, 6 out of 20 gave their own family name after the company's name. In the American speech community, 19 events concerning institutional and door-to-door sales were recorded. However, all of the salespeople who belonged to the aforementioned categories knew the customers well. As a result it is impossible, in this research, to compare the way in which the salesmen identified themselves in the speech communities. However, a highly successful American salesman explains the importance of the use of the personal name in the American speech community.

He (prospective customer) walks in the front door, and the first thing I say is, 'Hi, my name is Joe Girard.' And the very next thing I say is not, 'What's your name?' I don't want to scare him any more. I don't want him to start pulling back right away. So, instead of asking, I say, 'And your name is...' He won't hesitate a second before he finishes that sentence and tells me his name... It was natural and casual, and I got his name. From then on, I use it, because we now have a personal relationship. He's Bill and I'm Joe. And if he tries to call me Mister, I let him know that it's Joe (Girard 1977:158).

The following anecdote about an American high school girl's encounter with a door-to-door salesman indicates the important role of the personal name in American society (personal communication). One day, the student and her grandmother were at home. Suddenly, they heard the doorbell ring. The girl saw a man standing outside the door. He said that he was selling vacuum cleaners from door-to-door and asked if they were interested. They refused, however, to let him in until he gave them his own name. The two examples just cited show that the Japanese salesman identifies himself by indicating the company to which he belongs rather than by giving his own name, but that

American salesmen as well as customers consider the personal name more important in the identification procedure.

4.2.2 Middle

4.2.2.1 Approach. After the initial opening stage of the sales transaction, salesman and customer proceed to the next stage, 'approach'. This is a transitional stage from simple mutual exchange of greeting to the actual stage of initiating the business transaction. In both speech communities, two approaches can be observed: (1) the 'may-I-serve-you' approach and (2) the 'merchandise' approach (Wheeler 1941). The 'may-I-serve-you' approach is initiated by the salesperson only, while the 'merchandise' approach can be initiated either by the salesperson or by the customer.

Approach	Initiated by
'may-I-serve-you'	salesperson
'merchandise'	salesperson customer

4.2.2.1.1 'May-I-serve-you' approach. In the 'may-I-serve-you' approach, the contact to get into the business transaction between the salesperson and the customer is initiated by the salesperson's address to the customer. Some examples of this approach from the data collected are given in (21) through (25).

(21) S: May I help you?
　　 C: I would like to get a...box of candies.
　　 S: All right. (AC department store)
(22) S: Can I help you?
　　 C: Thank you. We're just looking.
　　 S: Right, OK. (AC department store)
(23) S: Do you need some help (F)?
　　 C: I'm already being helped. Thank you (F). (JC department store)
(24) S: Someone is helping you?
　　 C: Yeah. (AC department store)
(25) S: Are you being waited on?
　　 C: No, I'm waiting for my friend here. (AC flea market)

The surface structures of (21) and (22) are interrogative, but from the context it is understood that both (21) and (22) are not enquiring about the salesman's ability to help the customer, but are the salesperson's offer to help the customer. In other words, both utterances (21) and (22) are interrogatives in form, but are offers in function. Utterance (23), on the other hand, is interrogative in form. It is a request for information as well as an offer to help the customer. Utterance (24) is a statement with an interrogative intonation, and again this utterance is an offer in function. Utterance (25) is interrogative in both form and function. Like utterance (23), it also includes an offer of assistance. Thus, by means of various patterns of offer and question, a possible transaction is opened by the salesman.

4.2.2.1.2 'Merchandise' approach initiated by salesperson. Another approach is the 'merchandise' approach, which is characterized by a reference to the merchandise made by either the salesperson or the customer. The difference from the 'may-I-serve-you' approach is that the 'merchandise' approach leads directly to the initial business transaction without an introductory utterance about salesperson's willingness to serve the customer or about customer's intention of buying a specific item. Rather, either salesperson or customer indicates something of value about the merchandise the customer has in mind. This can be initiated by the salesperson, as in examples (26) through (29).

(26) S: We are selling jewelry, clothing, furniture, and everything you want. (AC flea market)

(27) S: So, welcome, welcome to your facials. MK's (brand's name) skin care, MK's essential skin care, essential skin care if you want a lovely beautiful complexion. That's what MK's about and it's a fine products system. (AC door-to-door)

(28) S: It (cosmetics) gives you the look you see in magazines and not something you don't see. Want to try it?
C: OK. I'll try it.
S: Take a seat. I'm glad you are here. (AC department store)

(29) S: Would you like a sample?
C: Thank you. What is it?
S: DC (name of the perfume company) fragrance.
C: Oh, that's nice.
S: They're having a makeup show. This is a nice gift to give. It has the famous D. This one is nice for travel. (AC department store)

Examples (26) and (27) are introductory statements to attract customers' attention to the merchandise. Example (26) is an invitation to activities in the flea-market and (27) is an explanation given by the cosmetic door-to-door saleslady to the prospective customers. Both (26) and (27) are the salesperson's appeal to the crowd or group who are interested in the merchandise. Therefore, there is a pause after the salesperson's introduction and the customer's immediate response is not observed. Example (28) is an interaction between salesman and customer. First of all, the salesman tries to invite the customer to his cosmetic studio so that he can give a facial. The customer agrees and takes a seat. The saleslady in (29) initiates her utterance by offering a sample of perfume instead of approaching the customer with the 'may-I-serve-you' technique. The customer agrees to accept the sample and the saleslady explains about the perfume and its merits. All the data in examples (26) to (29) were collected in the American speech community. Similarly, the 'merchandise' approach can be observed in the Japanese speech community, as in examples (30) through (35).

(30) S: Well, as I already explained (HM) to Dr. A (H) about this, I would like to talk (H) to you about this medicine today (F). (JC institutional)

(31) S: I am (HM) sure that you already know (H) (F) because this is being advertised by the television these days (F) (2). Sewing machine by which we sew any kind, thick or thin material (F). (JC institutional)

(32) S: Welcome, welcome! Such a tasty and nice looking melon for only 500 yen. (JC street hawker)

(33) S: I know (HM) that you are very busy (H) but today I would like to explain (H) to you about the raw materials of (company's name) (F). (JC institutional)

(34) S: Please try (H) to taste. It's good. I'm sure you like (H) it (F). (JC private store)

(35) S: Well, frankly speaking (HM), I'm very sorry to trouble (H) (you) (F), but I am visiting (HM) to explain (H) about the insurance (F). (JC door-to-door)

The salesman in (30) initiates his interaction by explaining that the customer is not the first and only one to listen to him about that merchandise but that he has already had a chance to talk with another doctor. By so doing, he seems to try to convince the customer that he is obliged to listen to him. The salesmen in (33) and (35) apologize for their visit before introducing the business of the day. In (31), the salesman begins to explain about his merchandise, a sewing machine, by making the customer aware of the mass media advertisement about the merchandise, as well as by explaining its advantages. Example (32) is a description of the merchandise by a street hawker. In (34), the saleslady tries to call attention to the food she is selling by offering it to the customer. Thus, except for examples (32) and (34), the salespeople make introductory remarks before engaging the customer in business talk.

It seems that when Japanese salespersons employ the 'merchandise' approach, they are liable to give preliminary remarks which may serve to establish a harmonious relationship before initiating business talk directly. Here again, as in the greeting technique, it is the salesperson in the Japanese speech community who tries to be concerned about the customer's situation and interests.

4.2.2.1.3 'Merchandise' approach initiated by customer. In some cases, a customer initiates the business transaction. This can be achieved in three ways: (1) by requesting information about the availability of the item the customer would like to order or to buy, (2) by simply asking where the customer can find the merchandise, and (3) by requesting the item from the salesperson at the serving post. A customer initiates the interaction of business with the salesman by the first method as shown in examples (36) and (37).

(36) C: Do you carry this brand?
     S: Oh, yes, we do (F). (JC private store)
(37) C: I would like some information. Does D (brand's name) come in size 8?
     S: We get very little. (AC department store)

Examples of the second method are given in (38) and (39).

(38) C: Where are the batteries?
     S: (pointing the direction) Right in the direction you're heading. (AC private store)
(39) C: Could you tell me in what section I can find men's shirts (F)?
     S: Right here, sir (H). (JC department store)

Finally, examples (40) and (41) illustrate the third method, in which the customer requests the item from the salesperson.

(40) C: I would like a set of handkerchiefs.
     S: Certainly (HM), here it is (F). (JC department store)
(41) C: Could you price these out?
     S: OK. (JC institutional)

These interactional conversations between customer and salesman form another adjacency pair, that is, request-compliance. In each situation, a customer requests in the first utterance and the salesperson complies with the request in the second utterance. However, in some cases, the salesperson would like to affirm the customer's request instead of complying immediately. In these cases, the salesperson repeats the item requested by the customer. This kind of technique, which is called playback (cf. Merritt 1977), is of two kinds: assertive and query.

Examples of assertive playback are given in (42) and (43).

(42) C: Is there Saran Wrap?
      S: Saran Wrap. Yes (F), (walks to the other corner
          of the store). I'll get (HM) you some (F).
      C: Thanks. (JC private store)
(43) C: Top (brand name of a soap).
      S: Top, all right (HM) (F). (JC private store)

Here, the salesperson repeats the name of the item requested
without any question intonation. The purpose is simply to reaffirm the customer's intention. However, examples (44) and (45)
are somewhat different from (42) and (43).

(44) C: Well, O (name of medicine).
      S: Isn't it a pill that you want (F)? Right?
      C: Yes, that's it. (JC private store)
(45) C: *Kami sori* 'a straight-edge razor'.
      S: *Kami sori* for a woman (F)?
      C: Yes. (JC private store)

These examples indicate that the salesperson would like to get
further information for clarity and reassurance or to provide a
chance for correction when he repeats the name of the item which
the customer has already requested. Hence, these are query
playbacks and the data indicate that these playbacks are always
accompanied by question intonation. Although each has a distinct purpose, both kinds of playback have important functions:
(1) they provide an opportunity for the customer to correct
errors, if any, and (2) they confirm the salesman's willingness
to attend faithfully to the customer's need and request.

4.2.2.2 Negotiation

4.2.2.2.1 Structure and procedure. The data indicate
that, at the negotiation stage, there are three main procedures:
(1) directing attention, (2) persuasion, and (3) satisfaction.
In the first, the salesperson attracts customers' attention in
order to arouse interest in the merchandise. In the second, he
(1) leads the customer to become aware that the merchandise is
necessary for him, (2) makes him realize and believe that the
merchandise fulfills his requirements, and finally (3) urges the
customer to make the merchandise his own. Finally, after taking
the customer's order, the salesman insures the customer's satisfaction by supporting his decision to buy. In case the customer
decides, after the negotiation procedures, to refuse the merchandise, the direct business talk is terminated. The negotiation procedures are outlined in Figure 4.14.

Figure 4.14 Negotiation procedures.

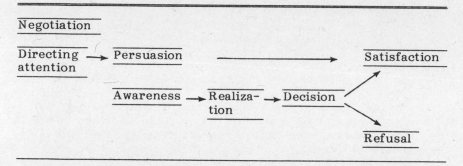

4.2.2.2.1.1 **Directing attention.** In the directing attention stage, the salesperson, after finding out the prospective
customer's need at the earlier 'approach' stage, calls the customer's attention to the merchandise which the salesperson recommends. The following interaction between a salesperson and a
customer illustrates this stage. The data, collected in the
coat section of a department store, are from the American speech
community.

(46) S: Here's a nice one exactly like that one. (C
          shows a little hesitance). What's wrong with this?
          Single breasted with the raglan sleeve and a little
          collar. Isn't that perfect? It's just like the
          picture (which customer had) Look!
      C: The collar is a little bit...

4.2.2.2.1.2 **Persuasion.** Here, S tries to convince C that
the merchandise she recommends is the best, and to lead her to
buy it. The data continue in example (47).

(47) S: OK, honey, you are not going to get something
          like that (pointing at another one).
      C: I know...(hesitantly).
      S: I mean it is the same type of a collar and the
          sleeves are perfect and it is single breasted. You
          can't get nicer than that.
      C: (nods) Huh, huh.

S once again explains how nice the coat looks, makes C aware of
its suitability, and assures her that she will not be able to
find nicer merchandise. Evenutally, then, S. persuades C to buy
it.

(48) S: I think it is lovely for her.
      C: That is a real white one, isn't it?
      S: No, that's an off-white, I think. Actually that
          is a nice color. I think that is what she would

like. I think that is what she would want, that
shade. It's the nicest.
C: Yeah...
S: It's a nice looking coat. I would imagine that's
the coat she had in mind, don't you?
C: OK, I'll get this.

4.2.2.2.1.3 Satisfaction. After S successfully persuades
C to purchase the merchandise, she affirms C's decision by making an encouraging remark. Thus, the event continues:

(40) S: You did good today. You did good today.

4.2.2.2.2 Discourse strategies. The discourse strategies
salespersons use can be classified as nonverbal or verbal. The
nonverbal category includes human behavior such as eye contact,
nod, friendly smile, etc. Verbal strategy includes paralinguistic and prosodic cues such as intonation, stress, rhythm, sentence speed, etc. Linguistic strategies also have a very important function in this category. In this research, emphasis
is placed on linguistic aspects of discourse strategies, because
it is very difficult to observe, record, and analyze nonverbal
behavior and present the results in detail without appropriate
facilities such as videotape. Paralinguistic and prosodic cues
can generally be studied by playing back the recorded tapes over
and over again. In this instance, however, it would be difficult to arrive at a final result because most of the tapes were
recorded in a natural situation and there are many background
noises and instances in which two or three people talk simultaneously. After careful observation and analysis of the data, it
became obvious that the following linguistic strategies play an
important role in sales transactions: (1) strategy of repetition, (2) strategy of exaggeration, and (3) code-switching.
These are discussed in section 4.3.

4.2.3 Closing

4.2.3.1 Pre-closing. Pre-closing is the stage after the
negotiation has been terminated, when either the salesman or the
customer gives signals that he is ready for leave-taking. Data
collected in the American speech community indicate that the
following are typical markers of pre-closing: *So, all right,
OK, Here we are, Hokey-doke, There you go, Thank you so much,*
etc. These are shown in examples (50) through (61).

4.2.3.1.1 Initiated by salesman.

(50) S: So (with downward intonation contours)
      C: You're finished for the day?
      S: That's it. (AC institutional)

(51) S: Well, thank you for the order.
      C: OK. (AC institutional)
(52) S: All right.
      C: OK. (AC flea market)
(53) S: Thank you very much.
      C: Thank you. (AC individual store)
(54) S: All right. I'll bring it to you next week to
          let you try it. OK.
      C: OK. Thank you. (AC institutional)
(55) S: Thank you so very much. I hope it all works out
          for you.
      C: I hope so.
      S: Right. (AC department store)
(56) S: All right, John. I thank you sir.
      C: I guess that's about it.
      S: OK. (AC institutional)
(57) S: OK. Thank you.
      C: Thank you. (AC department store)
(58) S: Here we are. Enjoy. Thank you very much.
      C: All right. (AC department store)
(59) S: Thank you. That's 49 out of $60.00. Here's
          $11.00 and your receipt and thanks so much.
      C: You're welcome. (AC department store)
(60) S: Well, you're not mad at me any more, are you?
      C: No.
      S: OK. I thank you. (AC institutional)
(61) S: OK. I'll check with you then.
      C: OK. (AC institutional)

Careful study of these pre-closing formulas confirms that
utterances like *thank you, all right, OK,* play dual functions as signals and also as expressions of gratitude or affirmation. The criterion for distinguishing the function is basically the position of the utterance in the exchange. The first
appearance is usually a signal and when the utterance is repeated by either party, it connotes gratitude, affirmation, or
agreement. The outline of the data is as follows.

Formula:

S's signal + C's affirmation + S's agreement. See (50).
S's signal + gratitude + C's agreement. See (51).
S's signal + C's affirmation. See (53).
S's signal + gratitude + C's gratitude. See (53) and (57).
S's signal + reference to future business + C's agreement +
    gratitude. See (54).
S's signal + wish for customer's satisfaction + C's agree-
    ment + S's agreement. See (55).
S's signal + gratitude + C's affirmation + S's affirmation.
    See (56).

S's signal + wish for customer's satisfaction + gratitude + C's agreement. See (58).

S's gratitude (finish business) + gratitude + C's (conventionalized) welcome. See (59).

S's affirmation that the customer's complaint has been solved + C's agreement + C's signal + gratitude. See (60).

S's signal + promise for future business + C's agreement. See (61).

4.2.3.1.2 Initiated by customer. In some cases, a customer takes the initiative in pre-closing, as shown in examples (62) through (64).

(62) C: Thank you very much.
　　　　S: All right. (AC individual store)
(63) C: OK. Well, thank you very much.
　　　　S: You're welcome, I'm sure. (AC department store)
(64) C: OK.
　　　　S: Thank you very much. (AC department store)

Formula:

C's gratitude + S's agreement. See (62).
C's signal + gratitude + S's (conventionalized) welcome. See (63).
C's signal + C's gratitude. See (64).

The foregoing data suggest that the basic pattern of pre-closing includes two, three, or all of the following four elements: (1) signal, (2) affirmation, (3) agreement, and (4) gratitude. The basic pattern is extended to include various elements like reference to business, wish for customer's satisfaction, and assurance that the customer's complaint has been solved.

In regard to the signals of pre-closing which are commonly found in the data from the Japanese speech community, these may be freely translated by expressions that are equivalent to those already enumerated in the analysis of data from the American speech community, e.g. *So, all right, OK,* etc. In the discourse of Japanese door-to-door salesmen, however, these signals are ordinarily followed by expressions of great formality, deference, and courtesy which lengthen the utterance considerably and make this type of transaction much more ornate and ritualistic than its counterpart in the American speech community. Some of these expressions, together with a rather literal English gloss, are listed here.

(a) *Yoroshiku onegai itashimasu* 'I request that you will take care of me in the way you think fit.'

(b) *Ojama itashimashita* 'I have disturbed you'. This expression is used when one visits someone whose time one has taken up considerably.

(c) *Mata oukagai sasete itadaki masu.* *Oukagai sasete* is a humble form of 'to visit'. The literal meaning is 'I would like to visit you again.'

(d) *Dōmo sumimasen deshita* 'I am unable to make up for the trouble I have made.'

(e) *dōmo.* This word can have many meanings if it is used by itself. It can be used by either the salesman or the customer. Literally, it means 'really'; in context it conveys: (1) '(an apology for one's rudeness)', (2) '(a signal of thanks for a service rendered)', (3) '(a word of thanks for the trouble and labor involved)', (4) a remark of consent. Thus the exact meaning of the term depends on the immediate context but because the expression is conveyed indirectly, it always conveys a subtle and somewhat indefinite meaning.

As has already been observed in the American speech community, in most cases it is the salesman who initiates the pre-closing. The interactional pattern of pre-closing within the Japanese speech community reveals an abundance of stereotyped conventionalized expressions. Some examples of these conventionalized formulas are as follows:

Formula:

S's signal (a)(d)(b)(e[1]) + C's affirmation.
S's signal + gratitude + C's agreement (d) (e[3]).
S's signal + a + C's agreement + S's (d).

These formulas are noninterchangeable, and nonreciprocal. They are definitely conventionalized patterns which may be used exclusively by the salesman. This usage is very different from the less formal, more creative approach that was observed in the analysis of data from the American speech community. In addition, the usage of lexicon is also conventionalized in the sense that door-to-door salesmen frequently use the following vocabulary.

hitotsu. Literally, it means 'one item'. Then when the salesman adds as he usually does, *Yoroshiku onegai itashimasu* (the expression just explained in (a) of the immediately previous list), he is emphasizing that he really has one desire: that the customer will take care of him and listen to his request in the near future.

mata. Literally, it means 'again'. It is used as 'I would like to visit you again', 'I will request again that you will treat me in the way you think fit', 'I will disturb you again', and so forth. It is one of the techniques the salesman uses to keep contact with the customer even after the business transaction of that day is over.

tokoro. Literally, it means 'when'. The salesman usually uses it in apologizing to the customer, 'when you are very busy', or 'when you are tired', etc.

4.2.3.2 Leave-taking. Leave-taking is the period of terminal exchange between salesman and customer. In the American speech community, adjacency pairs like *goodbye/bye, OK/OK, thank you/you're welcome* are often used. The data indicate that the following terminal exchanges are repeatedly used between salesman and customer.

(65) S: Bye, have a nice day (Thanksgiving, weekend, or vacation).
      C: You, too. (thank you)
(66) C: We'll be seeing you on (Thursday, Monday, etc.).
      S: All right. Thank you.
      C: Bye, bye.
(67) S: OK.
      C: OK. (Bye)
(68) S: I'll be back (thank you).
      C: Bye.
(69) S: OK. I thank you.
      C: OK. All right, bye, bye.
(70) S: So long (C's first name). I'll see you (next week). I thank you for this nice order today.
      C: So long (S's first name). Have a nice week.
(71) S: Thank you. Come again.
      C: All right.
(72) C: That's OK.
      S: OK. Thanks a lot. Bye, bye.

As was observed in the data, in addition to the adjacency pairs just mentioned, sometimes the comment and wishes for spending the weekend or a special holiday (65), invitation to visit the store again (71), and remarks for future business (66), (68), and (70), are included in the leave-taking exchange. These wishes for having nice holidays and remarks regarding future business are used either by salesman or customer, and thus these formulas can be reciprocal between them. As another characteristic of the interactional pattern of leave-taking in the American speech community, expressions like *OK, all right, thank you* are frequently repeated after either salesperson or customer has already used them in pre-closing.

In the Japanese speech community, in addition to the expressions cited in 4.2.3.1.2 (a)-(e), which are frequently used in the pre-closing section between the door-to-door salesman and the customer, the following formulas are also observed, particularly in leave-taking.

(f) *Dōmo shitsurei itashimashita.* Here, *dōmo* is used at the beginning of a sentence as an emphasizer. It may be translated 'indeed', 'really', or 'very much'. The whole expression literally means 'I was really impolite to have disturbed you'.

(g) *Ja, gomen kudasai. Gomen* means 'pardon (me)' and it is used any time a speaker asks pardon. In leave-taking, therefore, it means 'pardon me for leaving'. *Ja* is a signal that the speaker is ready to leave.

(h) *Gokurō sama.* Literally, it means 'hard work' and the whole sentence means 'it was hard work.' This is used when one appreciates the effort of a person who is in one's employment or a person from whom a service can reasonably be expected.

One of the differences of the leave-taking speech pattern between American and Japanese speech communities is that Americans express terminal exchange by (1) thanking each other, (2) wishing each other a happy day, (3) commenting on the business transaction, and (4) referring to a future business transaction. In contrast, the Japanese speech pattern of leave-taking is less informal, more ritualistic, nonreciprocal, and lengthy due to the abundant courtesy formulas which are traditionally prescribed. The exchange between salesman and customer in the American speech community is characterized by freedom of expression, while in the Japanese speech community, the role expectation is so definite that spontaneity is limited. With regard to the different types of sales transactions other than door-to-door sales, the data indicate that the terminal exchange is simpler and shorter, as examples (73) through (75) show.

(73) S: Thanks again (F).
C: Thank you for your care (e[3]). (JC private store)
(74) S: Come (H) back again, please (F).
C: Pardon me for leaving. (JC department store)
(75) S: Well, take care (H) of yourself (F).
C: Thanks. (JC department store)

The common feature of this speech pattern and that of the door-to-door sale is that the salesman always uses honorifics when he talks to the customer and the customer usually answers in plain forms. The only exception to this usage can be found in the speech of street-hawkers or salesmen in open markets. This reveals another basic difference from the speech pattern of the American speech community: in the American speech community, regardless of the different situations, the terminal exchange is freely used by the salesman or the customer without effecting any change in the basic pattern. Both salesman and customer seem to be more friendly and to cooperate with each other in a more informal atmosphere. Thus, the basic and typical patterns of leave-taking are reciprocally used by salesman and customer in an effort to create a friendlier and more flexible relationship with each other.

4.3 Linguistic strategies for presentation and negotiation

4.3.1 Strategy of repetition. Data in both speech communities sometimes uses the same expression or same word over and over again to emphasize some point during conversation with the customer, especially at the stage of negotiation. For example, it can be seen from the data in section 4.2.2.2.1.2 that these expressions are repeatedly used by the coat salesperson.

(76) You can't get nicer than that.
It's the nicest.
It's a nice looking coat.
(77) I think that is what she would like.
I think that is what she would want, that shade.
(78) You did good today,
You did good today.

Examples (76) and (77) refer to the coat which S is recommending and the third expression is used when S tries to help C feel satisfied about the purchase of the coat. Sometimes, S uses the same vocabulary repeatedly to emphasize a specific aspect of her explanation. The cosmetic door-to-door salesperson in the American speech community talks as in example (79) in order to explain that soap is bad for washing the face.

(79) S: Of course, you know you never, never, never, never use soap. (AC door-to-door)

In the Japanese speech community, this strategy is frequently used in a long narrative by door-to-door salespersons regardless of the kind of merchandise they carry. We already observed this point in Chapter 3 in the data dealing with the door-to-door salesman who is selling a sewing machine. Similar characteristics can be seen in the following data which record a sales transaction in which a door-to-door salesman is selling a globe.

Points emphasized   *Frequency*

Point 1.   necessity of having a globe   14 times
Point 2.   inexpensiveness of purchasing   16 times
           by monthly installment

During the course of a door-to-door sales transaction in the
Japanese speech community, the strategy of repetition is employed very skillfully. The salesman switches the subject to a
different topic for a while and comes back again to emphasize
the point, and if this does not seem to work he goes back to the
former topic from a slightly different angle and repeats the
same point again. This strategy may indicate that the salesman
has nothing more to say than to explain the same points over and
over, but it is more likely that, through this technique, the
salesman expresses his intention not to retreat from his position.

4.3.2   Strategy of exaggeration.   This strategy is frequently used in both speech communities when the salesperson
talks about the merchandise he is offering.   Usually, this
rhetorical strategy is accomplished (1) by the use of specific
adjectives   in   the   positive   degree   like   *attractive,   nice,
lovely, perfect, super, cheap, terrific,* uttered with strong
intonation,   and   (2)   by   the   use   of   these   adjectives   in   the
superlative degree.   From the data observed in this section,
Here's a nice one exactly like that one and *I think it is
lovely for her* are examples of the first strategy.   Examples
of the second strategy are given in (80) and (81).

(80)   S: Isn't it pretty?   And made in the good USA.
       C: Yeah.
       S: Which is nice.   These are *best*.   (AC depart-
            ment store)
(81)   S: Today is the day when you can shop (H) cheapest
            (F).   Only today is opened (F).   Only today is
            opened. Everybody (H) knows (H) about this super
            bargain sale.   Today is the last day when you can
            shop (H) cheapest in a super bargain sale.   (JC
            private store)

As example (81) indicates, the strategy of exaggeration is sometimes combined with the strategy of repetition within the same
utterance in order to produce a better effect.

4.3.3   Code-switching.   In   the   data   collected   in   the
Japanese speech community, code-switching is observed in several
places.   The type of code-switching which is used is that of
alternating between the honorific or polite form and the plain
form.   The following data provide an example.   The participants
are a door-to-door salesman and a customer who is a housewife.

The salesman is trying to sell a globe to the customer, explaining that a monthly installment plan is very convenient and economical. From the beginning of his talk, his speech pattern is characterized by the use of honorifics and polite forms when he refers to the customer, and plain or humble forms when he refers to himself. However, in a certain situation, his speech pattern is not consistent; namely, he employs code-switching, as in example (82).

> (82) S: I hear (HM) that the parents (H) spend (H) about
>   15,000 or 20,000 yen on children (H) (F). How
>   about you (H)? How much money are (you) (H)
>   spending for your children (F)? Well, for your
>   (H) children (H).
>   C: 25,000 or 26,000 yen.
>   S: Well, it is what everybody (H) does (H) (F).

The salesman uses the word *children* three times: with honorific suffix, without honorific suffix, and with honorific suffix again. The first time he mentions *children*, he refers to parents of children in general. As he wants to show respect to the parents to whom he is speaking, he uses the honorific suffix for children. Prior to this utterance he has explained that he himself is the father of a son, and therefore he intuitively thinks of the customer and of himself as on an equal basis. Thus, when he asks the customer about the amount of money she spends for her child, he uses the plain form of the word *children* as he refers the word to his own children. However, he soon realizes that it refers to the customer's children and switches from plain to polite form in order to express respect toward the addressee.

Another example of code-switching between informal and formal style is seen in example (83). The paticipants are a salesperson and a customer. S is selling eyeglasses and contact lenses in a private store. He is about 27 years old and C is a high school girl about 17 years old. After the stage of 'approach', S initiates the business transaction.

> (83) S: Is this a first time that you (H) buy (H) eye-
>   glasses (F)?
>   C: Yes.
>   S: Is that so (F)? Please try (H) these three (F).
>   I think (HM) you (H) may like (H) this kind (F).
>   C: How about this kind?
>   S: Well, could (you) wait (H) for a moment (F)?
>   (S picks up the house phone to ask a fellow salesman
>   about the eyeglasses C has just requested.)
>   S: Is there 0 and -1 over there? Yes, we have? I
>   want that. I will get that.
>   (   )
>   All right.

(S goes back to C.)
S: (to C) I hear (HM) that we have that kind (F).
    If you (H) wait for ten minutes, we (HM) will make
    (HM) that for you (H) (F).

As indicated in the data, S's speech pattern shifted from formal
to informal style without any honorifics or humble forms when he
talked to his own fellow salesman. However, when he returned to
C, he again switched to the original speech pattern, that is,
polite forms with honorifics referring to C and humble forms
referring to himself consistently in formal style. This investigation indicates that it is most likely that code-switching in
the Japanese speech community is firmly linked with the salesman's sensitivity regarding whom he is addressing and whom he is
talking about.

4.3.4 Basic principles of negotiation

4.3.4.1 Role relationship. In order to grasp the whole
picture of how the salesperson tries to persuade the customers
in each speech community, it is necessary to observe the interactional conversation in sequence between salesperson and
customer. For this purpose I refer again to the data already
described in Chapter 3: (1) a cosmetics sale in an American
department store (Section 3.4), and (2) a door-to-door sale of a
sewing machine in the Japanese speech community (Section 3.5).
    With regard to the data from the American speech community,
the process of negotiation can be outlined as follows.

1 U 79   S: What you need is . . .
          C: (no chance to talk, just listening)
2 U 79   S: Do you want to try some of that foundation,
             the beige one?
   U 80   C: No, I want to think about it.
3 U 81   S: You don't want anything, not even a lip-
             stick?
   U 82   C: No, I think I want to see how this feels for
             a while.
4 U 87   S: Why don't you get the lipstick?
          C: (no direct reply.)
5 U 94   S: The lipstick you should have for yourself.
   U 95   C: Yes, I have lipstick.

After S succeeds in selling the new lipstick, he still continues:

6 U 100 S: ...you should come back for these.
          C: (no direct reply)
7 U 108 S: I don't know why you don't get that rouge.
          C: (no direct reply, but shows her own lip-
             stick).

8 U 114 S: You don't want to get your makeup?   The blush?

   U 115 C: I'm going to think about that.   I might be back later.

9 U 116 S: Not even the blush?

   U 117 C: I might be back later.

10 U 125 S: You should get some of that treatment.   I have a lot of it (presenting a booklet).

   U 126 C: I'll be back when I know what I want.

As can be seen from this interaction, the role relationship between salesman and customer is one of equality.   Each person presents his/her own opinions forthrightly.   (1) The salesman keeps suggesting that the customer buy the products even after she has refused.   (2) In the course of conversation, he even employs vocabulary items equivalent to giving an order to the customer, using *need* and *should* four times.   (To me, a nonnative speaker of English, this repeated use of *need* and *should* seems excessively coercive on the salesperson's part and therefore impresses me as impolite usage.   Perhaps not all Americans would agree with my interpretation, and this would be another proof that language is indeed culturally conditioned.) (3) At the first and second invitation to buy, the customer refuses clearly and directly, giving some reasons why.   (4) Three times the customer does not respond directly to the salesman's invitation but talks about a related topic.   (5) Three times she does not say a direct *no*, but instead mentions that she may come back when she knows what she wants.   Throughout the tenth negotiation procedure, each side seems to work out his/her own task.   The salesman tries to convince the customer that she should be aware of the necessity of makeup creams, etc., and that she should decide to buy them.   The customer, on the other hand, clearly expresses her feeling that she is reluctant to buy the products, except the lipstick: (1) she wants to see how the cosmetics already applied by the salesman will affect her skin and appearance; and (2) because of this, she does not know what she really wants to buy, at least at that moment.   Thus, the salesman as well as the customer discusses from his/her own point of view.   Therefore, the conversation is carried on in a situation of real confrontation.

In the Japanese speech community, the negotiation procedure seems to be somewhat different from what has just been observed in the American speech community.   First of all, in the data on the door-to-door salesman and the customer in the Japanese speech community, expressions like *Yes, I can see, Is that so?*, or simply *hum, hum* are frequently used by both participants.   Second, the speech pattern of the salesman is characterized by the consistent use of honorifics and polite forms.   Third, the Japanese salesman never uses expressions like those of the American cosmetic salesman, repeated here as examples (84)-(87).

(84) You don't want...
(85) Why don't you get...
(86) I don't know why you don't get.
(87) You should get...

Instead, the Japanese salesman recommends the sewing machine more indirectly and politely, using the following expressions.

U 27: ...I think you need to use this at home...
U 39: . . . Then, for your daughter's marriage, how about one?
U 49: ...If you pay a deposit, I can bring you the one.
U 53: However, if you say that you need a sewing machine, you can take it.
U 55: How about one when your daughter marries?
U 75: Maybe, it is the time for your daughter to marry and it will be good for that preparation.
U 109: Well, I thought it good for your daughter.

Fourth, the salesman never refuses directly what the customer answers but just responds with *hum, hum* or *Is that so?* Finally, his speech pattern is filled with postpositional particles like *ne, desuga,* and *yo,* each of which serves a special function in a special situation (cf. Section 4.3.4.2). The customer also strives to understand the salesman's point of view by answering *Yes, I can see* or simply *hum, hum.* Even if she wants to refuse to buy the sewing machine, she does not mention the refusal directly or clearly. Rather, she assumes that the salesman will interpret her indirect way of speaking as refusal. The following examples illustrate her indirect manner of refusal.

U 34: Therefore, there is no way...
U 54: However, we don't use it at our house...
U 56: We'll think of it, that time...
U 70: ...We already have one. Therefore...
U 72: One machine can do anyway...
U 106: Well, I will consider it, again.
U 108: Hum, besides, we have one already.
U 122: But we already have one.
U 124: ...Well, I will think of it, so...
U 126: I can't decide so suddenly.

Another characteristic of the expression of indirect refusal is that, in many cases, it begins with some conjunctions or hesitation marks, such as *therefore, besides, however, but,* and *well.* This indicates that the customer tries to refuse indirectly but not forthrightly.

These characteristics of negotiation procedure in the Japanese speech community indicate the following underlying social norms of behavior: (1) a salesman in the Japanese speech community always uses polite forms and honorifics to show respect to the customer, and communicates his own views indirectly and with great sensitivity; (2) although the customer does not use polite honorific forms in speaking to the salesman, she too is polite, especially when she intends to refuse the salesman's invitation to buy. Thus, the direction of the conversation is a mutual attempt to create a harmony minimizing the real confrontation. This underlying aspect of the Japanese way of negotiation can be more thoroughly investigated through careful study of the various functions of postpositional particles used by salespeople in the Japanese speech community.

4.3.4.2 Use of postpositional particles. Postpositional particles in Japanese are used at the end of utterances and serve two general functions: (1) as markers to signify the speech pattern of either male or female; and (2) as markers to indicate the informality in the utterances. Some postpositional particles are *zo, ze, ya, na, yo, sa, ne, wa* and *daga, zo, ze, ya,* and *na*, which are used predominantly by males, while *wa* and *no* are used by females. It is interesting to observe in the data collected in the Japanese speech community that in some cases of postpositional particles, the restricted use by sex is neutralized and the particles are used by either male or female. It is even more interesting that, although postpositional particles serve as markers to introduce informality to the utterance, they play still more important roles in the conversation between a salesman and a customer. The postpositional particles used frequently by salesmen are *ne, keredo,* and *desuga,* regardless of the salesperson's sex. Of these three particles, *ne* is used most frequently, as shown in Chapter 3. Another postpositional particle *keredo* is used for indirect expression of preference so as not to impose the salesperson's will on the customer. More specifically, this particle serves to express the salesman's subtle desire to share his intention and judgment with the customer and still not to force his opinion completely. Some of the examples from the data are as follows:

(88) S: I think it does not matter, since it is made of 5 grams... *keredo* 'but'... (F) (JC institutional drug sale)

(89) S: Well, I would like to explain (H) a little. I think you will understand (H) if you read (H) it *keredo* (F). (JC institutional drug sale)

(90) S: This frame is better *keredo* (F). (JC private store)

(91) S: I will talk (H) with the doctors (H) *keredo* (F). (JC institutional drug sale)

(92) S: This (H) looks much better *keredo* (F). (JC department store)

(93) S: I think you (H) like (H) this much better and I
          do think (HM) so *keredo* (F). (JC department
          store)

Another postpositional particle *desuga* 'it is so...but' is
used by a salesperson in order to entrust the final decision to
the customer, instead of expressing his own feeling directly and
forthrightly. The following examples show how a salesperson
tries to accomplish this function.

(94) S: I think this is better, *desuga* (F).   (JC
          private store)
(95) S: It will be good, if you (H) come (H) to our
          store *desuga* (F). (JC private store)
(96) S: I think it will come out. I think you (H) will
          understand *desuga* (F).
(97) S: This is a sample *desuga*.   (JC institutional
          drug sale.
(98) S: I think this one is more convenient (H) for you
          desuga (F). (JC door-to-door)

It is obvious that these particles function to avoid conflict of
opinions and to create a harmonious atmosphere in which the
salesman can express his own views and intentions indirectly and
sensitively.

4.3.4.3 Speech level and honorifics

4.3.4.3.1 Verbal inflection and prefixes on nouns. Every
language has a certain way to convey polite expressions. For
example, a native speaker of English knows that *Could you do
this...?* or *Would you mind doing...?* is stylistically more
polite than *I want you to do...* Similarly, when a speaker
is asked to explain about his friend at a job interview, everybody knows that he does not use the word *guy*, but *my
friend* or *Mr.* in reference to his friend, since the situation is rather formal and serious. Thus, the interpersonal
relationship between speaker and hearer, and the situation in
which the conversation is carried on, determine the speaker's
choice of specific speech patterns, plain or polite expressions.
Accordingly, a sentence may change its form syntactically, mor-
phologically, and phonologically. The great difference from
Japanese, however, is that in English there is no stereotype
formula between the interpersonal relationship and polite,
honorific expressions. In English, for example, when the speaker *I* wants to give this book to the addressee *you*, the
utterance is *I will give you this book*, regardless of the
relationship which exists between speaker and addressee.
In Japanese, on the other hand, there are strict rules of
verbal inflection and prefixes on nouns, depending on the social
status, age, sex, occupation, etc. of the participants involved

and the social situation in which the utterances are issued.
Thus, if the speaker is in a lower status than the addressee,
the verbal inflection of 'give' *sashiageru* is used. If the
speaker is in a somewhat equal status with the addressee, the
verbal inflection is *ageru*. *Yaru*, on the other hand, is
used when the speaker is in a higher status than the addressee.
Similarly, the noun for 'book' also takes different forms according to different situations. If a speaker is in a higher
status or older than the addressee, he does not add any prefix
to the noun *hon* 'book', but if a speaker is in a lower
status or younger than the addressee, the prefix *go-* is
added to the noun for 'book', hence *gohon*. Example (99)
illustrates the contrasting Japanese expressions used by a
Japanese speaker when he is of lower status (-), equal status
(=), or higher status (+) than the addressee.

(99) (-) Kono gohon o sashiagemashō
this book (object-marker) give-will
'I will give you this book.'
(=) Kono hon o agemasho
this book (object-marker) give-will
'I will give you this book.'
(+) Kono hon o yaru
this book (object-marker) give-will
'I will give you this book.'

It is clear from this example that verbal inflection and
prefixes on nouns are shifted from one form to the other
according to the different interpersonal relationship between
speaker and addressee. In the case of interaction between
salesman and customer, the relative power relationship of the
speaker and hearer is always observed; with the exception of the
sales at the market and street hawkers, the data indicate that
the salesman consistently uses polite forms and honorifics with
the customer, regardless of the age and social status of the two
parties.

4.3.4.3.2 Lexical choice. In addition to the frequent
use of polite expressions and honorifics, the data also indicate
that a salesman chooses specific terms during face-to-face en-
counters with the customer. Some of the examples of lexical
choice are as follows. Instead of mentioning 'inexpensive', the
word *oneuchi* meaning 'honorific + worth' or 'honorific
value' is used. When the salesman must refuse the return of
already purchased goods, he uses *go yōsha* meaning 'honorific
+ forgiveness'. Also, a euphemism is occasionally used to
avoid hurting the customer's feelings. For example, when an
insurance salesman explains the terms of payment, he uses this
special technique as follows: *In case of your husband's
emergency, you will receive...* rather than saying *the death
of your husband*. As a technique to refuse a customer's

request indirectly and more politely, the salesman adds certain phrases like *zannen nagara* 'to my regret', *fuhoni nagara* 'reluctantly', *oainiku sama desuga* 'honorific + unfortunately', and *sekkaku no omōshide desuga*, meaning 'honorific + in spite of your special request'. Thus, careful use of special lexical choice is another means the Japanese salesperson uses to exhibit consideration for his customer's situation and point of view.

4.3.4.3.3 Violation of discourse rule. As noted in Chapter 3 and in this chapter also, the salesman's talk with the prospective customer in the Japanese speech community is characterized by the frequent use of polite expressions, honorifics, and the careful choice of lexicons, euphemisms, and the addition of specific phrases in order to be polite to the customers. This characteristic can be applied to the various types of salesmen's talk except to sales at the market and by street hawkers within the Japanese speech community. Example (100) is taken from a sales event at the market in downtown Tokyo. The salesman, who wears a headband and shirt with short pants, is selling grapes.

(100) S: Do you think that you can buy these elsewhere? Seedless, aren't they? (to the customers who have tasted the produce) Consider, you can't buy this kind anywhere. You can't buy it!

Example (101) is from a street-hawker who is selling fish on a street corner in Tokyo. The salesman wears a headband and bellyband with short pants.

(101) S: Listen! You're crazy if you don't buy it! Take my advice!

The common feature to be observed in (100) and (101) is that the salesman seems to put great pressure on his customers. His manner of address is to holler. The syntactic structure of his utterance is characterized neither by polite expressions nor by the use of honorifics. Moreover, his statement and his speech pitch are far from the gentle and polite approach of the salesmen observed in other types of sales transactions, such as door-to-door sales, institutional sales, sales in department stores and private stores, etc. In short, these data indicate that the patterns of salespersons at the market and of street hawkers violate the discourse rule. The violation can be recognized first of all by the verbal usage. Both street hawkers and salespersons at the market use plain forms for 'buy' and do not modify the verbal inflection of that form to show respect for customers as the other types of salesmen do. Second, they speak to the customers in command forms instead of using an indirect invitation to buy. Nevertheless, it seems that, through the violation of the discourse rule, salesmen assume an important role and by doing so, have an unusual effect upon their customers. Thus, violation of the rule of courteous address seems to be an accepted technique of street hawkers and salesmen at the market. The customers apparently enjoy the role reversal in this type of business transaction, as can be seen by their response of nodding, smiling, and finally purchasing the proffered merchandise. The role reversal means that, in the ordinary type of transaction, the customers take for granted that they will be treated with politeness and that the salesman is the one who listens patiently to the customers' opinions and impressions. Hence, the relative power in the relationship between the street hawkers and salespeople at the market, and the customers, is also reversed in this specific type of business transaction. In short, salesmen give an order to customers and customers listen to it and obey the salesmen's request.

4.3.4.3.4   Different levels of formality.   It is obvious that the Japanese language has a definite system of polite expressions and the fundamental relationship underlying the honorific system is the relative power of the speaker and hearer in any transaction. It is clear that in business transactions in the Japanese speech community, the customer has more power and is treated with politeness by the salesperson. This fact is proven by the collected data in which salesmen talk to customers, using honorifics and polite expressions regardless of the customers' social, economic, and age status. Furthermore, careful study of the data indicates that polite expressions are used on different speech levels in different situations by the salesmen. If the salesman in the American speech community announces that he will deliver the requested merchandise to the customer, he says *I will deliver the requested merchandise to you.* However, in Japanese, there are three ways to express respect to the customers at different levels of formality:

(1) High formal: Go chūmon no oshinao otodoke itashimasu
(honorific)   requested   noun-modifier
(honorific) + merchandise (honorific) +
delivery (honorific) + make

(2) Plain formal: Go chūmon no oshinao otodoke shimasu
(honorific)   requested   noun-modifier
(honorific) + merchandise (honorific) +
delivery (honorific) + make

(3) Low formal: Go chūmon no oshinao otodoke shimasu yo
(honorific)   requested   noun-modifier
(honorific) + merchandise (honorific) +
delivery (honorific) + make (conclud-
ing-marker-for-insistence)

Utterance (1) has the highest degree of formality, and (2) and (3) represent decreasing levels of formality. The three examples explain the various ways of using polite forms which express respect to customers in (1) the high formal, (2) plain formal, and (3) low formal speech levels. The critical distinguishing features among these forms are verb endings and the additional use of postpositional particle. The same principle may be demonstrated with the use of humble forms. In Japanese, when a speaker, talking with an addressee of higher social status, refers to himself, he uses humble forms. This principle can also be applied to the relationship between salesman and customer. When the salesman wants to communicate to the customer that the salesman himself will deliver the merchandise, he explains by one of three expressions using humble forms of the verb 'bring' at different levels of formality:

(1) High formal: Shinamono o motte agarimasu
                   requested-merchandise object-marker (humble) + being (humble) + go
(2) Plain formal: Shinamono o omochi shimasu
                   requested-merchandise object-marker (humble) + bring (humble) + do
(3) Low formal: Shinamono o omochi shimasu yo
                  requested-merchandise object-marker (humble) + bring (humble) + do (concluding-marker-for-emphasis)

Although the three utterances are at different levels of speech, they all express humble feelings toward the customers, the first being the most humble, and the second being more humble in expression than the third.

4.3.4.3.5 Variable factors. Section 4.3.4.3.4 shows that Japanese salesmen, with very few exceptions, treat customers with extreme courtesy. This attitude is manifest in the consistent choice of polite speech styles for conversation with customers. Section 4.3.4.3.4 also shows that courtesy and humble forms can be used on different formal levels of speech. My next concern is to investigate the variable factors which determine the hierarchy of polite expressions. One of the prior findings of this study is that in public address at the market, at the department store, and on a train, the salesperson consistently employs formal-formal style. The common features shared by these three systems of public address are: (1) it is always directed from a certain physical distance, (2) it is addressed to a crowd in general rather than to specific individuals, and (3) it is addressed through a microphone. Consequently, the salesperson and his audience are mutually out of sight. Taking the three foregoing factors as tentative variables, I move to the next task, that of examining the data in which one of the variables appears and making a comparison with other data which lack the specific variable. First of all, I analyze two events in which the salesman speaks (1) from a distance and (2) in face-to-face encounter. Similarly, I consider a salesman's address directed (1) to a group in general and (2) to an individual customer. Finally, I investigate a salesman's address (1) when the customer is out of sight and (2) when the customer is readily visible.

The first example is taken from the salesman's speech at a private establishment. The physical disposition of the store is as follows: the room is large and deep; the seller is located at the rear of the store on a platform; the merchandise is displayed on long counters at either side of the store. When the salesman issues his invitation to buy, he is at a relatively great distance from the prospective customers. (To differentiate the three formal styles in the data presented in (102), the following symbols are used: (HF), high formal; (PF), plain formal; (LF), low formal.

(102) S: Please drop in (PF). We are waiting (H) for your (H) coming (PF). Right now, we are welcoming (H) you (H), having a large assortment of various goods in stock (HF). Shirts, summer sweaters, one-piece dresses are all worth buying (H) (HF). Please look at (H) the items (PF). We have a complete stock of items (HF), in response to your (H) everyday support (H) (PF).

Example (103) presents a conversation between a salesman and a customer at another private store. The physical situation is different from that described in example (102). The salesman and his customer are in close face-to-face contact.

(103) S: Welcome (PF)!
C: Well, sun cream.
S: Certainly (PF). Well, this is 500 yen and the other is 1200 yen (PF).
C: What do you call this? Is this like jelly (PF)?
S: Yes, you can use (H) it as a foundation for your facial (LF). I think this is more effective on your skin (PF). I think it is better if you want (H) to use (H) it for going out (LF).
C: Can I use it for foundation, also?
S: I can imagine yes (PF) but this is oily, you know (LF). This is all right if you use it for (your) face (H) (PF).
C: Can I use it for my skin (LF)?
S: Oh, sure (PF) indeed (LF).
C: I will get this.
S: Thank you (PF).

Both examples (102) and (103) show that polite forms are used by the salespeople. However, the salesman in example (102), who speaks to his customers from some distance, uses predominantly plain formal style with occasional instances of high formal style. He never employs the low formal style. The salesperson in example (103), on the other hand, is engaged in a face-to-face encounter with his customer and his speech is characterized by the frequent use of plain formal style, with occasional instances of low formal. He never uses high formal style.

The conversation in (104) was also recorded in a private store. In front of the store, the salesman tries to attract the customers' attention. He is addressing the group in general, not specific individuals.

(104) S: Please come (H) in without hesitation (H) (PF) and look at (H) the various items in our store (PF). Any item is worth buying (H) (HF). Thank you so much for (your) coming (H) (HF). Welcome, welcome please come (H) in (PF). We are serving you (H) in a greater stock of everything you request (H) (PF) for your size and design (HF). We are very happy to find a good one which is becoming to (H) each of you (PF). There is not any other store except this one which is serving (HM) you by such a worthy price (HF). Please, please...

(He continues the general invitation for everyone to enter the store and shop.)

Each utterance of this salesman's talk is marked by a polite expression. The verbal inflection and prefixes on nouns are consistently used to show respect in the plain formal or high formal speech level.

Example (105), taken from the data, records the interaction between a saleswoman and a customer in a private store in a shopping mall. The saleslady is selling a hair curler and addresses a woman who approaches.

(105) S: Hi, lady (H), well, please buy one more (LF). It's very simple to use (LF). Just push the bottom (PF). I'm always using this (LF). Please buy one (PF). You can set your (H) hair for only 700 yen (LF).
C: Can I buy only one?
S: Sure, but I know that you will like it (PF) so, why don't you buy (H) two now (LF)?
C: I don't know yet, if...
S: Certainly, you can begin (H) by trying one for your hair (PF). It's very simple to use (LF). I can recommend any kind to you (LF).
C: Is this smaller than this (LF)?

S: Yeah. Maybe, you can use (H) it for your hair
(PF). I also use this kind on the top of my head
like this (LF). See, but if you have two, you
have no worry how to take care (H) of your hair.
Besides, this is the last day for the sale, you
know (LF).

C: Well, I really don't know if this is good for
my hair or not (LF).

(The negotiation between saleswoman and customer continues.)

The saleslady's speech pattern is characterized by polite
forms and the postpositional particles which signify women's
speech and the informal speech level. On the other hand, when
the salesman addresses his customers as a group, he talks in
either the plain formal or high formal levels but never uses
postpositional particles which are indicative of low formal
style.

Example (106) is the sales announcement delivered to customers
on each floor of a department store in Tokyo.

(106) Thank you so much (H) for coming (H) to the department store today (HF). Right now (H), (we) are having big bargain sale of various kinds of undershirts
(H) for summer (HF) at the special entertainment
place on the 8th floor (HF). (We) are having a large
assortment (H) of various kinds of undershirts (H) in
stock ranging from gentlemen's (H) sizes and women's
(H) sizes to children's (H) sizes of famous brands
like U (brand's name), K (brand's name) and R
(brand's name) and some other bargain brands for the
comfortable (H) summer (HF). At the same time, (we)
are having a big bargain sale of all kinds of bags
(HF). (We) are waiting (HM) for your (H) coming
(HF).

The statement through the public address system is consistently marked by polite expressions on the high formal speech level.
In addition, use of *Kango* is scattered throughout the message. As has already been discussed (Section 4.1.8), this usage
always conveys especially courteous expressions. The data in
(107) are different from the data in (106) in the sense that the
speech pattern is not in a high formal speech level, even if the
utterance is filled with polite expressions. The salesperson is
selling food, newspapers, and magazines on the train and visits
the passengers in each coach to bring them this merchandise.

(107) S: How about ice-cream (PF)? Coffee (PF)? and
sandwich (LF)?

C1: Give me a sandwich (LF).

> S: Yes, 100 yen (PF)   (S receives money and con-
>   tinues to sell) How about coffee (PF)?
> C2: Give me *shūmai*.
> S: *Shūmai?*   It comes with the lunches (H)
>   (LF).
> C2: Give me coffee then (PF). How much is that?
> S: 230 yen. Thank you (PF).

The salesperson uses polite forms but the speech level is either plain formal or low formal style.

From these investigations, it is clear that (1) distance, (2) number of customers, and (3) the invisibility of the customers are important factors in deciding which speech level is chosen in the salesman's talk within the Japanese speech community. Namely, the data indicate the following points: (1) salesmen's talk is more polite when they keep a certain distance from the customer than when they are in direct interaction with the customers; (2) salesmen talk more politely to a group than to each person separately; (3) salesmen's talk is most polite through the public address system (a) when there is a certain physical distance between salesman and customer, (b) when the message is addressed to a sizable number of customers, and (c) when the customers are invisible to the salesperson.

4.3.4.3.6   Signals of polite forms.   No kind of speech exists independently of the situation in which it occurs. As a result of careful observation of sales transactions and analysis of data, the following can be identified as the signals when the salesperson is about to use honorifics, polite forms, and specific words and special phrases to pay deference to the customers.

(1) When the salesman is requested by the customer to answer something, he chimes in with customer's remark by adding *ha* in a lower pitch once or twice. This *ha* serves as a marker to indicate that polite expressions will follow.

(2) When the salesman himself asks some questions of the customer, the salesman makes the insufflated sibilant slit fricative noise [ss] (reminiscent of the sound made in sipping hot tea). This [ss] also functions as a signal to introduce polite expressions.

(3) The expression *yoroshiku* 'I hope you will kindly look after us' is not itself a polite expression, but serves as a marker for following expressions which are always polite.

(4) When the salesman is dressed neatly with tie and suit, he always uses polite forms and honorifics. Therefore, there is a correlation between the salesman's appearance and the manner of his speech.

4.4   Use of address forms.   The use of address forms is a feature which has special importance throughout all stages of the data currently under investigation. This aspect of usage reveals another contrast between the American and Japanese communities. In Japanese, all address forms are nonreciprocal. When address forms are used in the flow of conversation, they are always used with polite forms during sales transactions. Address forms are used with a polite suffix such as -san, -sama or with honorific titles for specific occupations, such as Sensei for doctors and school teachers. Common address forms used in the Japanese speech community can be classified into seven types:

(108) Type of address form: Basic formula:

    (1) Kinship terms — (kinship term) + (honorific suffix)

    (2) Personal name — (personal name) + (honorific suffix)

    (3) Personal pronoun — (second personal pronoun)

    (4) Honorific title — (Sensei) 'teacher, doctor, etc.

    (5) General term — (guest) + (honorific suffix), etc.

    (6) Occupational title — (name of the occupation) + (honorific suffix)

    (7) Name of the store/firm — (name of the store/firm + (honorific suffix)

Examples of these types as found in the data are as follows. (The address forms in each utterance are italicized.)

Examples of Type (1):
    S: Kore, *okusama*, machigai gozaimasen.
    this Mrs.-Wife + (honorific) mistake (honorific) + not
    'There is no mistake (F), *Mrs. Wife*-(H).'
    (JC door-to-door)

    S: Hai, *onēsan*, ohayō!
    Hi sister + (honorific) good-morning
    'Hi, *sister*-(H), good morning!'
    (In Japanese, the term *sister* does not refer to family relationship, nor do the terms *aunt*, *mother* used in the following examples.)
    (JC street-hawker)

    S: Hai, irasshai, *obasama*, kyowa hanawa?
    Hi, welcome Mrs.-Aunt + (honorific) today how-about-flowers
    'Hi, welcome, *Mrs. Aunt*-(H), how about flowers today!'
    (JC market sale)

S: Hai, *okusan*, arigatō.
   Hi, Mrs.-Wife + (honorific) thank-you
   'Hi, thank you, *Mrs. Wife*-(H).'
   (JC street-hawker)

S: Mitete yo *okāsan* hora yoku kireru desho?
   Please-try-to-see (marker-to-attract-attention) mother
   + (honorific) look + (exclamation) well cut isn't-it
   'Please try to see this, mother-(H). It does cut
   well, doesn't it?'
   (JC market sale)

Example of Type (3):
   S: Omoshiroku nai yo *anta* atsukute sa.
      interesting not (marker-for-insistence) you (informal)
      hot (concluding-marker-for-stating-reason)
      'It's not interesting, *you*, because it's so hot.'
      (JC private store)

Example of Type (4):
   S: Sensei anō (medicine's name) no ken de A sensei ni
      ohanashishi te...
      Doctor + (honorific) well (medicine's name) noun-modi-
      fier matter-concerning Doctor A (object-marker)
      (honorific) + talk (connective)
      'Doctor (H), about the matter of (the name of the
      medicine), I would like to talk (H) with Doctor A.
      (F).'
      (JC institutional)

   S: *Sensei* mō oyasumi o toraretan desuka?
      Doctor + (honorific) already (honorific) + vacation
      (object-marker) (honorific) + take did?
      'Doctor (H), did (you) take (H) vacation (H) already
      (F)?'
      (JC institutional)

Examples of Type (5):
   S: Hai gotsūkochu no okyakusama kyō kagiri degozaimasu.
      Hi (honorific) + passing-away (noun-modifier) (hono-
      rific) + guests today only (honorific) + is
      'Hi, guests (H), (the sale) is (H) only today.'
      (JC private store)

   S: Anone, mō hitotsu katte kudasai, *okyakusama* ne.
      Well, more one buy please-do (honorific) + guests
      (marker-for-indirect insistence)
      'Well, please buy one more, *guests* (H).'
      (JC market sale)

Although most societies use personal names as address forms, this mode of address (type 2) is not common in Japanese business transactions and therefore is not observed in the data collected for this study. Likewise, examples of types 6 and 7 are not observed in the data. The fact that address forms from these two categories did not emerge from the data analysis was particularly surprising to me. As a member of the Japanese speech community, I fully expected to find numerous instances of this feature. In my experience, it is quite common usage to address categories of people by the occupation name with the honorific title like *Hokenya San* which means 'honorable Mr. insurance' or *Honya San* which means 'honorable Mr. bookstore.' It is also possible that the name of the store or firm with honorific suffix can be used as a direct address form, as with *Kōrindō San* when the salesman works in a company called *Kōrindō*.

In English, it is noticeable from the data that, in contrast to Japanese usage, personal names are often used in a variety of ways in business transaction. To begin with, the first name is usually used between salesman and customer if they know each other quite well or even in the early stage of their acquaintance (personal communication with several salespeople). Second, in the formal situation or at the initial stage of a business transaction, the last name is used between salesman and customer. Third, if salesman and customer have known each other for a long period of time, they use a diminutive form of the first name. As the data indicate, pet names (e.g. *honey*, *dear*, etc.) are also used, especially when a saleswoman addresses younger female customers. General terms and honorific titles are also used as in the Japanese speech community. Consequently, as the data show, address forms in the American speech community can be classified into six types.

Type of address form:	*Basic formula:*
(1) first name	first name only
(2) last name	title (Mr., Mrs., Miss) + last name
(3) diminutive name	diminutive name only
(4) pet name	pet name only
(5) general terms	general terms only
(6) honorific title	title only

Some examples from the data follow. The address forms are underscored.

Examples of Type (1):
    S: Dab it on your face first, <u>Barbara</u>.
       (AC door-to-door)
    S: <u>Marion</u>, is this the usual time sequence?
       (AC door-to-door)

S: Yeah, but it didn't have prices on it, Terry.
   (AC institutional)
S: John, how much is the mouse? That belongs to him over there.
   (AC flea market)
S: Hi-ya, Paul.
   (AC institutional)
S: OK, John, that's that.
   (AC institutional)

Example of Type (2):
S: How are you, Mr. O (last name)?
   (AC institutional)

Example of Type (3):
S: Otherwise, it looks like we're in pretty good shape, Deb.
   (AC institutional)

Examples of Type (4):
S: OK dear.
   (AC flea market)
S: Wait, let me get this out for you, honey.
   (AC flea market)

Examples of Type (5):
S: Pat it and gently, girls.
   (AC door-to-door)
S: Come in, folks.
   (AC flea market)

Examples of Type (6):
S: I thank you, sir.
   (AC institutional)
S: Thank you very much, sir.
   (AC institutional)

The data reveal that the use of address forms in the American speech community is reciprocal and the use of personal names is quite typical in business related conversation. The investigation of address forms in the two speech communities under consideration reaffirms the prior findings which have emerged from this research. The American inclination toward the reciprocal use of personal names between salesmen and their customers establishes a more relaxed and friendly climate for the transaction of business. The traditional usage in Japanese speech patterns for sales transactions precludes the use of first names. Japanese sales transactions, therefore, are executed in a more formal atmosphere in which the salesmen are always aware of the necessity of showing deference and respect toward their customers.

CHAPTER FIVE

ANALYSIS OF QUESTIONNAIRES AND INTERVIEWS

5.0   Introduction. In this chapter, principles of sales-personship are examined on the basis of (1) questionnaires for salespeople and customers and (2) interviews with salespeople in both speech communities under consideration.   A total of 85 American and 94 Japanese salespeople, and 86 American and 93 Japanese customers completed questionnaires.   Eleven American and 12 Japanese salespeople were interviewed.   Throughout the analysis of the data from these questionnaires and interviews, an occasional inconsistency is noted between the total number of respondents and the total number of replies to any one question. This is explained by the fact that some respondents chose not to reply to certain items.   In other instances, respondents pro-vided more than one reply to a given question.

It is important to state very clearly that the purpose and methods employed in this research were of a qualitative, not a quantitative, nature.   It is not the purpose of this research to project results from a statistically controlled study.

5.1   Analysis of questionnaires for salespeople. As ex-plained in Chapter 2, the questionnaire for salespeople con-sisted of six parts: (1) general information about salesperson; (2) examination of salespersonship; (3) qualities and skills as a salesperson; (4) sales technique; (5) use of address forms and speech patterns; and (6) sales attitude.   Detailed analysis of each category is presented according to this order.

5.1.1   General background. American and Japanese sales-people in this sample were very similar in most respects, in-cluding years of experience and educational background.   One significant difference was in age: 24 (28.3%) of the Americans were over 50 years old, while only 2 (2.1%) of the Japanese were in that range.   Types of salespeople also differed in the sample, with relatively more Americans who sell in stores represented, and relatively more Japanese who sell door-to-door or in other direct contexts.   This probably represents an actual

111

difference in the distribution of salespeople in the two communities, and not merely a sampling bias, but additional data would be needed to make this determination.

5.1.2 Examination of salespersonship. In the section on salespersonship, four questions are asked. The first is: 'To what degree do you pay special attention to your appearance?' Respondents are asked to indicate their answer on a five-point scale. The percentages of American (A) and of Japanese (J) who chose each point of the five-point scale are the following.

'great deal' vs. 'none at all'

	5	4	3	2	1
A%:	67.8	26.1	5.9	0	0
J%:	34.0	26.3	35.1	0	0

The results show that American salespeople are more conscious of their appearance than are their Japanese counterparts: 67.8% of the American salespeople answered that they pay great attention to their appearance, as opposed to 34.0% of the Japanese salespeople. In reference to the foregoing five-point scale, the average of the indicated response for Americans is 4.61; for Japanese, 3.87. This difference adds further emphasis to the observation.

The following question is also answered by checking one point on the five-point scale: 'To what degree do you think it important to study the sales product you represent?' In reply, 85.5% of the American salespeople and 83.5% of the Japanese salespeople indicated that they consider this very important. The distribution of the five degrees of importance and mean value indicated by the answers is as follows.

'great importance' vs. 'no importance'

	5	4	3	2	1
A%:	85.5	12.0	2.4	0	0
J%:	83.5	12.0	4.3	0	0

Examination of the average ($\overline{X}$) for Americans 4.83, and for Japanese 4.79 also shows there is less difference about the importance of knowing the product than about the importance of the appearance of the salesperson.

The third question of this section asks how salespeople identify themselves to customers. Respondents are asked to choose one answer from the following four categories:

1. By first indicating your name and then the name of your company (A%: 52.9 vs. J%: 2.1)
2. By first indicating the name of your company and then your name (A%: 6.4 vs. J%: 41.4)
3. By first indicating the name of your company and then

your name with your business card (A%: 4.7 vs. J%: 47.8)
4. Other (specify) (A%: 4.4 vs. J%: 0)
   4.1 Name of company and department (A%: 1.1)
   4.2 Handshake and name (A%: 1.1)
   4.3 Name card and name of company (A%: 1.1)
   4.4 Name only (A%: 1.1)

This question was not answered by 8.5% of the Japanese and 10.5% of the American salespeople, and 10.5% of the Americans mentioned that their type of selling does not require any kind of identification. The results show that 52.9% of the American salespeople identify themselves to their prospective customers by first indicating their name and their company's name, while 89.2% of the Japanese salespeople identify themselves by first indicating their company's name and then giving their own name (with or without a business card). This shows that Japanese salespeople consider the company of greater importance in identifying themselves. This is emphasized even more by the fact that, as shown in the summary, only 2.1% of the Japanese salespeople identify themselves by first indicating their name and then their company's name. In this sense, the company's name is the first priority before personal names in identifying salespeople in the Japanese speech community.

The last question in this section asks how salespeople consider the following six variables in a business transaction: (1) cost, (2) quality, (3) convenience, (4) appearance, (5) practicality, and (6) beauty: 'What are your priorities among these variables when you explain your product to the customer?'[1] Table 5.1 indicates the percentage of subjects in each

Table 5.1 Salesmen's priority regarding product.

Variable:	Percent of speech community:					
	A	J	A	J	A	J
	1st priority		2nd priority		3rd priority	
Cost	5.0	4.4	19.4	24.1	38.0	37.9
Quality	63.7	66.2	18.1	20.8	5.6	9.1
Convenience	13.7	12.3	12.9	30.7	11.2	20.6
Appearance	2.5	0	14.2	4.3	18.3	4.5
Practicality	12.5	16.8	32.4	16.4	22.5	24.1
Beauty	2.5	0	2.5	3.2	4.2	3.4

---

1. For clarification, 'appearance' refers to physical characteristics, size, shape, etc. of the merchandise, and 'beauty' refers to its pleasing quality or attractiveness; while 'practicality' and 'convenience' were considered separate attributes by most subjects, the distinction was questioned by others, and may be further clouded by the need for translation.

group that rated these variables as first, second, and third priority.

Table 5.2 The first three variables by salespeople.

Speech community:	American	Japanese
1st priority:	Quality	Quality
2nd priority:	Practicality	Convenience
3rd priority:	Cost	Cost

Table 5.2 recapitulates Table 5.1 according to the first three priorities in both speech communities. Table 5.2 indicates that in both American and Japanese speech communities, quality has first priority for salespeople in their negotiations with customers. However, salespeople in the two speech communities have divergent views as to the second priority. American salespeople consider practicality their second priority, while Japanese salespeople consider convenience second in importance. Table 5.2 indicates that salespeople in both speech communities agree that cost is the third priority.

At this point, it is interesting to consider customer response to the same question: 'Among these variables, what are your priorities in purchasing the product?' Customer opinion is indicated in Table 5.3. Customers' order of priority in making a purchase is illustrated in Table 5.4.

Table 5.3 Customer's priority regarding product.

Variable:	Percent of speech community:					
	A	J	A	J	A	J
	1st priority		2nd priority		3rd priority	
Cost	17.7	14.7	46.4	24.4	18.6	36.8
Quality	64.5	56.8	23.8	16.6	12.0	10.5
Convenience	1.2	10.2	1.1	33.3	16.0	25.0
Appearance	6.3	1.1	13.0	0	12.0	1.3
Practicality	6.3	17.0	11.9	25.5	28.0	23.6
Beauty	3.7	0	3.5	0	13.3	2.6

Table 5.4 The first three variables by customers.

Speech community:	American	Japanese
1st priority:	Quality	Quality
2nd priority:	Cost	Convenience
3rd priority:	Practicality	Cost

Evaluation of the earlier results on the same questions to salespeople and Tables 5.3 and 5.4 regarding customer response reveals the following points:

(1)   Salespeople and customers in both speech communities agree that quality is the most important variable in selling and buying.

(2)   American customers consider cost the second most important variable after quality, but Japanese customers consider convenience second.

(3)   Japanese customers as well as Japanese salespeople share the same order of the first three priorities in buying and selling products, that is, quality, convenience, and cost.

(4)   Although the second and third priorities of salespeople and customers are reversed, American salespeople and customers also agree that quality, cost, and practicality are the three most important variables in selling and buying.

(5)   'Appearance' and 'beauty' are low for both speech communities.

Table 5.5 indicates the first three priorities of salespeople and customers in both speech communities.

Table 5.5 Priorities of salespeople and customers with regard to product.

Priority	American Salespeople	Customers	Japanese Salespeople	Customers
1st	Quality	Quality	Quality	Quality
2nd	Practicality	Cost	Convenience	Convenience
3rd	Cost	Practicality	Cost	Cost

5.1.3   Qualities and skills of salesperson. This section changes the focus of the questionnaire by concentrating not on the sales product, but on the qualities of the salesperson who seeks to present the product convincingly. This is a departure from the area of materially oriented consumer facts into the area of personality--an area which is obviously difficult to measure.

Salespeople are asked to indicate on a five-point scale the importance of the following 11 qualities of a salesperson: (1) appearance, (2) manner, (3) speech pattern, (4) persuasiveness, (5) friendliness, (6) tolerance, (7) kindness, (8) consistency in personality, (9) enthusiasm, (10) ability to discern customers' response, and (11) honesty and sincerity. The responses were as follows.

The salesperson's views

Quality		'very important' vs. 'not important at all'				
		5	4	3	2	1
1. Appearance	A%:	68.2	27.0	2.3	2.3	0
	J%:	29.7	31.9	32.9	4.2	0

2.	Manner	A%:	82.1	13.0	3.5	0	0
		J%:	59.1	24.7	16.1	0	0
3.	Speech pattern	A%:	43.3	22.8	20.4	1.2	12.0
		J%:	54.8	25.8	17.2	1.0	1.0
4.	Persuasiveness	A%:	42.3	28.2	22.3	3.5	3.5
		J%:	76.3	11.8	10.7	0	1.0
5.	Friendliness	A%:	78.8	12.9	8.2	0	0
		J%:	42.3	32.6	20.6	1.0	3.2
6.	Tolerance	A%:	77.6	16.4	5.8	0	0
		J%:	31.8	30.6	29.5	7.9	0
7.	Kindness	A%:	58.8	2.1	15.2	4.7	0
		J%:	51.6	24.7	21.5	2.1	0
8.	Consistency in personality	A%:	61.7	22.2	12.3	2.4	1.2
		J%:	52.2	22.2	22.2	3.3	0
9.	Enthusiasm	A%:	73.4	21.6	3.6	0	1.2
		J%:	75.2	19.3	5.3	0	0
10.	Ability to discern customers' response	A%:	70.8	18.9	6.3	0	3.7
		J%:	60.2	26.8	10.7	2.1	0
11.	Honesty and sincerity	A%:	78.7	17.5	3.7	0	0
		J%:	65.2	23.9	10.8	0	0

The mean value ($\overline{X}$) for each of the same characteristics is as follows.

1. Appearance (A 4.61/J 3.84)
2. Manner (A 4.73/J 4.43)
3. Speech pattern (A 3.84/J 4.32)
4. Persuasiveness (A 4.02/J 4.62)
5. Friendliness (A 4.70/J 4.09)
6. Tolerance (A 4.71/J 3.86)
7. Kindness (A 4.35/J 3.86)
8. Consistency in personality (A 4.40/J 4.23)
9. Enthusiasm (A 4.66/J 4.69)
10. Ability to discern customers' response (A 4.53/J 4.45)
11. Honesty and sincerity (A 4.75/J 4.54)

Customers were also asked to use the same five-point scale to indicate their ranking of the same 11 qualities of a salesperson. Customers' responses are analyzed in section 5.2.

The customer's views

Quality		'very important' vs. 'not important at all'				
		5	4	3	2	1
1. Appearance	A%:	52.3	19.7	20.9	3.4	3.4
	J%:	22.4	31.4	40.4	3.3	2.2
2. Manner	A%:	87.2	9.3	3.4	0	0
	J%:	61.7	33.7	4.4	0	0
3. Speech pattern	A%:	32.9	35.2	25.8	3.5	2.3
	J%:	52.2	35.5	11.1	1.1	0
4. Persuasiveness	A%:	14.4	12.0	31.3	22.8	19.2
	J%:	57.7	17.7	16.6	5.5	2.2
5. Friendliness	A%:	55.8	27.9	16.2	0	0
	J%:	13.9	29.0	40.6	10.4	5.8
6. Tolerance	A%:	54.7	21.4	19.0	2.3	2.3
	J%:	23.5	32.9	31.7	8.2	3.5
7. Kindness	A%:	58.1	23.2	13.9	3.4	1.1
	J%:	48.3	29.2	15.7	4.4	2.2
8. Consistency in personality	A%:	44.0	21.4	23.8	8.3	2.3
	J%:	69.3	23.8	5.6	1.1	0
9. Enthusiasm	A%:	41.8	27.9	25.5	1.1	1.1
	J%:	69.6	6.7	12.3	10.1	1.1
10. Ability to dis- cern customers' response	A%:	65.1	22.0	12.7	0	0
	J%:	73.0	14.6	7.8	4.4	0
11. Honesty and sincerity	A%:	89.4	3.5	7.0	0	0
	J%:	82.4	13.1	2.1	2.1	0

The mean value (X) for each of the same characteristics for customers is shown here.

1. Appearance (A 4.18/J 3.66)
2. Manner (A 4.83/J 4.51)
3. Speech pattern (A 3.92/J 4.58)
4. Persuasiveness (A 2.79/J 4.23)
5. Friendliness (A 4.39/J 3.34)
6. Tolerance (A 4.23/J 3.64)
7. Kindness (A 4.33/J 4.16)
8. Consistency in personality (A 3.92/J 4.61)
9. Enthusiasm (A 4.08/J 4.33)

10. Ability to discern customers' response (A 4.52/J 4.56)
11. Honesty and sincerity (A 4.82/J 4.75)

The following points are of interest:
(1) As with salespeople, American and Japanese customers also differ in their opinions regarding appearance: 52.3% of the American customers consider appearance to be a very important quality in a salesperson, while only 22.4% of the Japanese customers share this view.
(2) Of the American customers, 55.8% regard friendliness as very important in a salesperson, but only 13.9% of the Japanese customers agree. Thus, to Japanese customers, both appearance and friendliness are only moderately important.
(3) Customers in the American and Japanese speech communities also differ in their views of speech pattern, persuasiveness, and tolerance. Examination of the mean value (X) substantiates the difference in viewpoints between the two groups. Comparison of responses from salespeople and customers in both speech communities provides the following conclusions:
(1) American salespeople and customers agree that a salesperson's appearance is very important.
(2) Japanese salespeople and customers consider appearance moderately important.
(3) The following is a ranking of important salesperson's qualities as seen by salespeople and customers in the American and Japanese speech communities. Ordering is in terms of the mean response of each group on the semantic differential.

American vs. Japanese salespeople

	A:	J:
1st	Honesty and sincerity	Enthusiasm
2nd	Manner	Persuasiveness
3rd	Tolerance	Honesty and sincerity
4th	Friendliness	Ability to discern customers' response
5th	Enthusiasm	Manner
Least	Speech pattern	Appearance

American vs. Japanese customers

	A:	J:
1st	Manner	Honesty and sincerity
2nd	Honesty and sincerity	Consistency in personality
3rd	Ability to discern customers' response	Speech pattern
4th	Friendliness	Ability to discern customers' response
5th	Kindness	Manner
Least	Persuasiveness	Friendliness

With regard to a salesperson's skills, the following question was asked: 'To what degree do you consider the following skills important as a salesperson?' A list of 10 skills was provided, with a five-point scale for the salesperson's response: (1) key words, (2) good grammar, (3) logical presentation, (4) fluency, (5) pronunciation, (6) facial expression, (7) tone of voice, (8) eye contact, (9) gesture, and (10) body posture. Responses indicated great diversity of opinion between the two speech communities.

Skill		'very important' vs. 'not important at all'				
		5	4	3	2	1
1. Key words	A%:	53.6	28.0	12.1	3.6	2.4
	J%:	44.9	32.5	19.1	2.2	1.1
2. Good grammar	A%:	65.4	23.4	9.8	1.2	0
	J%:	15.9	30.6	39.7	5.6	7.9
3. Logical presen- tation	A%:	68.2	28.0	2.4	0	1.2
	J%:	40.0	25.5	23.3	10.0	1.1
4. Fluency	A%:	54.2	31.3	10.8	2.4	1.2
	J%:	16.0	28.7	33.3	17.2	4.5
5. Pronunciation	A%:	54.8	30.4	13.4	1.2	0
	J%:	21.3	35.9	30.3	10.1	2.2
6. Facial expression	A%:	53.0	31.3	10.8	0	4.8
	J%:	33.3	44.4	13.3	7.7	1.1
7. Tone of voice	A%:	65.0	25.3	7.2	1.2	1.2
	J%:	24.1	39.5	28.5	7.6	0
8. Eye contact	A%:	70.7	18.2	4.8	1.2	4.8
	J%:	37.3	41.7	17.5	2.1	1.0
9. Gestures	A%:	40.2	34.1	15.8	4.8	4.8
	J%:	15.7	21.3	40.4	16.8	5.6
10. Body posture	A%:	55.1	25.6	17.9	0	1.2
	J%:	30.7	35.1	31.8	2.1	0

The mean value ($\overline{X}$) for each of the same characteristics is given here.

1. Key words (A 4.14/J 4.17)
2. Good grammar (A 4.53/J 3.29)
3. Logical presentation (A 4.62/J 3.93)
4. Fluency (A 4.34/J 3.34)
5. Pronunciation (A 4.39/J 3.64)
6. Facial expression (A 4.27/J 4.01)

7. Tone of voice (A 4.51/J 3.80)
8. Eye contact (A 4.48/J 4.12)
9. Gestures (A 4.00/J 3.24)
10. Body posture (A 4.33/J 3.94)

The responses indicated tht American salespeople consider good grammar, fluency, and gestures as very important skills for salespeople, but Japanese salespeople consider these skills of moderate importance. Moreover, pronunciation, tone of voice, and logical presentation are very important skills to American salespeople, while Japanese salespeople do not consider them important. These answers support the interview responses from salespeople. For example, an institutional salesperson (informant 2) from the American speech community commented on the use of good grammar as follows (see Tables 2.1 and 2.2 for information on informants):

I'm always aware of my English and pronunciation, since there are many poorly constructed English sentences and improper pronunciations used in our society.

This remark indicates the great sensitivity about grammar and the structure of English sentences. It is interesting that three of the Japanese salespeople (informants 1, 4, and 12) responded to the same question that although they consider good grammar an important skill, they believe:

If we have a spirit of service to others the customers will appreciate our behavior even if the grammar is not perfect. (Informant 1)

With regard to fluency, four salespeople (informants 3, 7, 9, and 11) in the Japanese speech community mentioned that they sometimes try not to speak fluently so that the customers will feel at home in talking and negotiating with them. Informant 9 states:

I do not try to speak fluently because if I am too fluent, the customers think that I am too proud. So, in order to show humility toward them, it is always better to be reserved. Therefore, I sometimes purposely speak stammeringly.

These comments show the different interpretations of American and Japanese salespeople concerning the two skills, good grammar and fluency.

The skills of salespeople, ranked according to their mean order of importance, are as follows:

	AC:	JC:
1.	Logical presentation	Key words
2.	Good grammar	Eye contact
3.	Tone of voice	Facial expression
4.	Eye contact	Body posture
5.	Pronunciation	Logical presentation

Both groups agreed that gestures were the least important.

5.1.4 Sales technique. The fourth section of the questionnaires deals with sales techniques. The first question is: 'Do you make specific preparation for a sales contact besides study of your product and personal appearance?' A positive reply was made by 55.2% of the American salespeople and 67% of the Japanese salespeople. Respondents who answered 'yes' were directed to specify the kind of preparation they usually make for a sales contact. Since this is an open-ended question, it is difficult to present all of the answers given. Careful analysis reveals, however, that answers from both the American and Japanese speech communities can be classified in five categories: (1) study competitive products with their merits and demerits, (2) determine availability and service of the product, (3) attend related meetings and conferences, (4) study customers' needs, and (5) study current topics in society. The first three categories are directly related to learning about different brands of similar products, and the fourth and fifth categories deal more indirectly with the actual selling process. Tables 5.6, 5.7, and 5.8 summarize the answers from the American and Japanese speech communities and indicate what kinds of answers are grouped into each of the five categories in the following pages. Percentages of salespeople who answered categories (1) to (5) in each speech community are shown in Table 5.6.

Table 5.6 Salespeople's response concerning sales contact.

Category	Speech community:	
	A%	J%
1. Competitive products	16.2	42.5
2. Availability and service	32.4	18.7
3. Meetings and conferences	5.4	3.7
4. Customers' needs	43.2	10.0
5. Current topics in society	2.7	25.0

The percentages uncover an interesting phenomenon: American salespeople make considerable preparation by analyzing customers' needs. Thorough preparation by Japanese salespeople consists of acquiring actual knowledge of competitive products, and also trying to be aware of world events and world news. This

Table 5.7 Preparation for sales contact by American salespeople.

Category:	
1. Study competitive products	1. Study reference 2. Prepare proposal and be ready to overcome objections 3. Do necessary fact-finding about other brands
2. Determine product availability and service	1. Get purchase order 2. Obtain sample proposals of type of service and product 3. Plan pre-approach mailing and telephone for appointment 4. Keep informed about sales 5. Write script or outline of presentation 6. Pre-plan demonstration 7. Keep informed about new fashion trends.
3. Attend related meetings and conferences	1. Take courses 2. Talk with other sales representatives on success and failures 3. Do market research
4. Study customers' needs	1. Attempt to learn as much as possible about prospects prior to call 2. Be familiar with clients' or prospects' life style and goals 3. Analyze clients' needs, ability to pay, and probable reactions
5. Study current topics in society	1. Study contemporary issues

characteristic of Japanese salespeople is closely related with how salespeople begin contact with a prospective customer. The difference between the American and Japanese viewpoints was elicited by the question: 'How do you initiate your conversation with your customer?'

Careful analysis of the answers to this question reveals that different salespeople have different forms of initial conversation with customers. Traveling salespeople in both speech communities said that they begin conversation with customers whom they know well by sharing current topics before initiating business talk. Salespeople in private stores or department stores in the American speech community welcome their customers

Table 5.8 Preparation for sales contact by Japanese
salespeople.

Category:	
1. Study competitive products	1. Study advantages and disadvantages of different brands 2. Study different products and their application 3. Study characteristics of one's own product not duplicated in competitive products
2. Determine product availability and service	1. Check merchandise stock prior to actual sale 2. Redecorate stores 3. Prepare pamphlets, brochures, and statistical data on products
3. Attend related meetings and conferences	1. Attend seminars and workshops 2. Discuss selling methods with other salespeople 3. Schedule regular meetings in which fellow salespeople can exchange opinions about selling
4. Study customers' needs	1. Study customers' hobbies, favorite topics 2. Study customers' family background (e.g. number of children)
5. Study current topics in society	1. Study topics like sports, economy, etc. 2. Cultivate common sense in many fields 3. Be aware of world events, including market and economic fluctuations

by exchanging greetings, by simply offering help, or by responding to the customers' requests. Data from the questionnaires supports the findings in Chapter 4 regarding the 'may-I-serve-you' and the 'merchandise' approach. Although the questionnaires indicate that the 'may-I-serve-you' approach is used more frequently than the 'merchandise' approach, there are various ways of initiating conversation with customers in the American speech community, as compared with the methods indicated in the questionnaires from the Japanese speech community. Some examples of the 'may-I-serve-you' and 'merchandise' approaches, taken from questionnaires completed by American salespeople, are as follows:

'May-I-serve-you' approach:
1. How may I help you?
2. Hi, may I be of service to you?
3. Good morning. Is there anything I can do for you?
4. Hello, how can I help you?

'Merchandise' approach:
1. Aren't these table cloths beautiful?
2. May I show you some ties or shirts?
3. Are you looking for a special color?
4. Hi, would you like to see a pair of sneakers today?

As to Japanese salespeople in private and department stores, the data show that they express welcoming remarks to the customers: *Irrashaimase* 'welcome (with honorific)'. This institutionalized expression contains cultural and social meaning, that is, this statement conveys not only greeting and a feeling of warm welcome, but also the spirit of readiness to offer help and service to the customers. Since most salespeople traditionally use this greeting, the questionnaire revealed little variety in response to this question. Table 5.9 illustrates how

Table 5.9 Initiation of conversation with customers.

Type of salespeople	Contents of initial conversation with customer	Percent A:	J:
Traveling and institutional	1. Current topics, world events, light talk, and gossip	4.4	22.9
	2. Weather	2.2	17.4
	3. The family and their interests and needs	8.8	16.5
	4. Inquiry about previous visit and previous business transaction	2.2	9.1
	5. Identification of themselves and/or their company	8.8	11.0
	6. Explanation of purpose of their visit	4.4	5.5
Store (private and department)	7. Greetings of the day and welcome	25.5	14.6
	8. Comment on customer's dress or appearance	4.4	0.9
	9. Explanation of what is on sale	5.5	0.9
	10. Offering help	33.3	0.9

salespeople in the American and Japanese speech communities initiate conversation with customers.

Table 5.9 shows that although both traveling and institutional salespeople in the American and Japanese speech communities begin their conversation with discussion of current world topics, light talk and gossip, the percentage among Japanese salespeople is much higher (22.9% as compared with 4.4% for the American salespeople). Another difference between the two speech communities is that they introduce these current topics for different purposes. Among the Japanese salespeople, three interviewees (informants 7, 9, and 10) explained that they try to spend some time chatting about books, movies, and other social and cultural activities in order to maintain a good relationship with their customers. Two American salespeople (informants 1 and 2) explained that at the initial stage of conversation with customers, they try to create a pleasant and informal atmosphere by making some general comments (about the pictures on the wall, etc.). They consider this kind of comment as a stepping-stone for moving on to a business transaction right away, rather than as a technique for having a good relationship with their customers. Table 5.9 also shows that in stores the Japanese initial greeting formula is very limited, while American initial greetings are more varied, including greetings of the day, welcoming remarks, offering help, etc.

The next question investigates how salespeople in the American and Japanese speech communities negotiate with their customers during the actual business transaction: 'How do you negotiate, that is, how do you reply to customers' objections, preferences for other brands of similar products, etc.?' Answers from salespeople in each speech community fall into seven categories of negotiation methods, as follows:

Method 1: Point out and insist on some better and unique qualities and advantages their own products have that other brands do not have.

Method 2: Show agreement instead of disagreement with customers, expressing empathy.

Method 3: Try to explain the situation as logically and coherently as possible.

Method 4: First listen to customer's objections.

Method 5: Smile and reply courteously so that the customer will be satisfied with the service during and after the sale.

Method 6: Let the customer recommend what he/she wants to see, and simply say 'If you are really interested in brand X, then why didn't you buy it?'

Method 7: Try not to create a heated discussion but foster a good atmosphere respecting customers' feelings.

Table 5.10 Methods of negotiation.

Method	Characteristics	Percent A:	J:
1	Emphasize advantage and superior qualities of their own products	46.4	17.0
2	Respect and agree with customers' objections	23.2	48.0
3	Cope with the situation logically and coherently	10.7	0
4	Let customers speak first	8.9	5.0
5	Emphasize service and show sincerity and kindness	7.1	4.0
6	Deal forthrightly with customers	3.5	0
7	Try to avoid confrontation with customers	0	16.0

Table 5.10 summarizes the negotiation methods used by American and Japanese salespeople.

Table 5.11 The first three priorities in negotiation.

Priority	Method: American	Japanese
1	1	2
2	2	7
3	3	1

Table 5.11 indicates each speech community's first three priorities among the methods of negotiation listed in Table 5.10. It is interesting that the first two Japanese priorities are concerned with human relationships rather than business orientation. It is also interesting that in the American speech community, method 7 is lacking, while Japanese salespeople consider it their second priority. The questionnaires show that American salespeople make no attempt to avoid confrontation with customers in negotiation procedures. Table 5.10 also reveals that method 3 and method 6 are lacking in the Japanese speech community. Japanese salespeople do not try to handle negotiation by explaining the whole situation logically and coherently, as in method 3. And, since they try not to cope with the situation directly, they do not try to overcome customers' objections by confronting the customers forthrightly (method 6).

The next two questions deal with how salespeople respond to customers (1) when they succeed in selling their merchandise, and (2) when they do not succeed. The answer to the first question has two time divisions: (1) immediately after the sale, and (2) shortly after the sale. The answers provided by salespeople in both the American and Japanese speech communities are summarized as follows.

1. Immediately following a sale:
   1.1 Express gratitude by words or behavior or both, and encourage repeat orders or invite the customer to come back (A%: 48.7 vs. J%: 77.9)
   1.2 Explain the follow-up service (A%: 17.9 vs. J%: 20.3)
   1.3 Congratulate the customer and rejoice with him (A%: 17.9 vs. J%:1.6)
   1.4 Request continued contact with the customer (A%: 15.3 vs. J%: 0)
2. Shortly after the transaction is over:
   2.1 Try to analyze why the sales transaction succeeded (A%: 57.1 vs. J%: 64.7)
   2.2 Try to keep a good relationship with the customer by sending a follow-up card (A%: 42.8 vs. J%: 17.6)
   2.3 Send a small gift of gratitude and visit the customer regularly (A%: 0 vs. J%: 11.6)
   2.4 Celebrate the successful sale with fellow salespeople (A%: 0 vs. J%: 5.8)

The items in sections 1 and 2 appear in the order of popularity. There was no response from the Japanese speech community on item 1.4 and no response from the American speech community on items 2.3 and 2.4.

The second question (how salespeople behave after failing to sell) can also be divided into two sections: (1) immediately after the sale contact and (2) shortly after the contact. The following is a summary of the answers to this question.

1. Immediately after the sale contact:
   1.1 Request prospects to reconsider the purchase and invite them to come back (A%: 61.2 vs. J%: 92.0)
   1.2 Thank customers for time and cooperation, and maintain a friendly atmosphere (A%: 19.3 vs. J%: 4.0)
   1.3 Give business card to customer (A%: 9.6 vs. J%: 4.0)
   1.4 Try to interest customer in other merchandise in the store (A%: 6.4 vs. J%: 0)
   1.5 Apologize and mention other stores where customer can find the product he is looking for (A%: 3.2 vs. J%: 0)

2. Shortly after the sale contact:
  2.1 Identify the reason why the sale was not made (A%: 57.1 vs. J%: 50.0)
  2.2 Reevaluate the data and arrange for another opportunity to persuade the customer (A%: 20.0 vs. J%: 15.0)
  2.3 Follow customer with phone calls, postcards, until he buys (A%: 20.0 vs. J%: 2.5)
  2.4 Begin new sales contact with different products (A%: 2.8 vs. J%: 2.5)
  2.5 Try to keep a good human relationship with customer until the next opportunity (A%: 0 vs. J%: 10.0)
  2.6 Try to visit customer occasionally (A%: 0 vs. J%: 10.0)
  2.7 Confer with top salespeople and get their advice (A%: 0 vs. J%: 10.0)

An interesting answer to this question found in the data from three American salespeople is 'follow up till they (customers) buy or die.' The sentence implies that these salespeople are business oriented. As noted in Table 5.11, Japanese salespeople seem to emphasize harmony with customers, especially through items 2.5 and 2.6, neither of which received a response by American salespeople.

With regard to closing the sales transaction, the following question is asked: 'How do you take leave of the customer?' (1) after a successful sale and (2) after no sale. A summary of the answers from American and Japanese salespeople follows.

1. After a successful sale:
  1.1 Show a great deal of enthusiastic appreciation (A%: 17.8 vs. J%: 84.4)
  1.2 Express thanks and add something else, e.g. 'Thank you and enjoy it', 'Thank you, have a nice day.' (A%:32.1 vs. J%: 6.4)
  1.3 Express thanks and request repeated order (A%: 28.5 vs. J%: 7.7)
  1.4 Congratulate customer on decision to buy (A%: 10.7 vs. J%: 1.2)
  1.5 Thank and encourage customer to keep in touch with salesperson (A%: 7.1 vs. J%: 0)
  1.6 Give name and phone number (A%: 3.5 vs. J%: 0)
2. After no sale:
  2.1 Apologize for being unable to satisfy customer's needs (A%: 27.5 vs. J%: 14.5)
  2.2 Express thanks for stopping by and taking time (A%: 24.1 vs. J%: 25.4)
  2.3 Invite customer to come back for any further assistance (A%: 17.2 vs. J%: 7.2)
  2.4 Try to direct customer's interest to other merchandise in store (A%: 10.3 vs. J%: 5.4)

2.5 Simply exchange greeting, such as 'Have a nice day' (A%: 10.3 vs. J%: 0)

2.6 Request customer to recognize merits and urge purchase of product, emphasizing that now is the best time to buy (A%: 6.8 vs. J%: 40.0)

2.7 Try to keep good human relationship for the next opportunity (A%: 3.4 vs. J%: 7.2)

In the questionnaire for customers, the following question is also asked: 'How do you take leave?' (1) after buying and (2) after not buying. When a customer takes leave after buying, two patterns are revealed: (1) the customer initiates the conversation after the transaction is over and (2) the customer responds to the salesperson's expression of thanks. When a customer initiates the conversation, the following expressions are indicated in the answers on the questionnaire.

1. Show thanks and appreciation (A%: 82.7 vs. J%: 50.0)
2. Express thanks and add some statement like 'Have a nice day' or 'Please take care.' (A%: 3.4 vs. J%: 12.2)
3. Appreciate and comment on salesperson's service (A%: 5.2 vs. J%: 20.0)
4. Check and ask about follow-up service (A%: 8.6 vs. J%: 17.7)

Some customers in both speech communities answered that it is always the salesperson who initiates the routine for closing a sale. As a customer's response to the salesperson's expression of thanks, the following speech patterns are observed.

1. You are welcome.
2. See you again.
3. Goodbye.
4. Thanks to you, I made a good choice.
5. Just leave without saying anything.

When customers do not buy, the following six closing expressions are shown.

1. Apologize for not buying (A%: 8.1 vs. J%: 30.5)
2. Express thanks for time, information (A%: 70.2 vs. J%: 30.5)
3. Ask salespeople to take care of them when they come back again (A%: 0 vs. J%: 11.7)
4. Express their intention to buy in the future (A%: 5.4 vs. J%: 17.6)
5. Ask salespeople to let them consider the purchase before actual buying (A%: 2.7 vs. J%: 4.7)
6. Simply respond to salespeople's statement with 'you are welcome', 'all right', etc. (A%: 2.7 vs. J%: 3.5)

7. Just leave without saying anything (A%: 10.8 vs. J%: 1.1)

From observation of these data concerning leave-taking between customers, it is clear that, in both American and Japanese speech communities, after the direct sales transaction is accomplished, thanks are exchanged and sometimes the conversation about the follow-up service is continued. Exchange of thanks is expressed in a variety of ways: for example, salespeople congratulate clients on their decision to buy, and at other times customers show appreciation for the help and information they have received from salespeople. As to customers' and salespeoples' responses to the question about what they do when customers do not buy, the data indicate that in both speech communities, expressions of thanks or apologies can come either from salespeople or customers. In both speech communities salespeople invite the customers to come back, and in both, customers show interest in coming back or reconsidering purchase of the product in the future.

The next question is: 'how do you discern whether or not the client is a prospective customer?' Responses to this question for both speech communities reveal four approaches:

1. By salespeople's intuition (A%: 10.7 vs. J%: 12.8)
2. By market research (A%: 10.7 vs. J%: 2.8)
3. By sizing up or analyzing the type of customer (A%: 28.5 vs. J%: 5.7)
4. By analyzing the customer's responses (A%: 50.0 vs. J%: 78.5)

According to the answers received, one way to discern whether or not the client is a prospective customer is by salespeople's intuition. One American salesperson who has been working in his selling field (clothing) for 25 years writes: 'intuition gained through experience.' Another way is by market research, that is, salespeople try to find out customers' work or leisure activities. On this basis, they discern a customer as a potential buyer. The third way to discern a customer is by 'sizing him up' through a series of questions to ascertain what he is really looking for and what his requirements are. Still another way is to discern from a customer's interest, attention, facial expression, and other responses to the salesperson's presentation. For example, Japanese salespeople list the positive signs of prospective customers as: (1) they ask questions seriously, (2) they pay careful attention to the explanation offered by salespeople, (3) they give positive responses to a sales pamphlet, and (4) they request samples, brochures, etc. The list of categories indicates that the most popular technique for discerning a prospective customer in both speech communities is based on the customer's response.

The last question under sales technique deals with the salesperson's method of convincing a customer to buy. The five principal methods are: (1) demonstration, (2) explanation of the advantage of the product, (3) presenting statistical results, (4) citing use of product by famous persons, and (5) comparison with competitive products or services. Results are given in Table 5.12.

Table 5.12 Priority of sales methods.

Method:	Priority by speech community:							
	A%	J%	A%	J%	A%	J%	A%	J%
	1st		2nd		3rd		4th	
Demonstration	35.1	19.3	37.5	20.8	10.1		4.4	12.1
Explanation	63.5	69.3	31.9	23.6	6.7	5.6		3.0
Statistics	0	6.8	16.6	18.0	54.2	35.8	22.2	24.2
Citing famous persons	0	0	4.1	5.5	3.3	5.6	22.2	39.3
Comparing with competing products	1.3	4.5	9.7	31.9	25.4	28.3	48.8	21.2

According to the list in Table 5.12, the order of priority of methods used by salespeople to convince customers to buy is as shown in Table 5.13.

Table 5.13 Priorities in selling techniques.

Priority	American	Japanese
1st	Explanation	Explanation
2nd	Demonstration	Comparison with competitive products
3rd	Statistics	Statistics
4th	Comparison with competitive products	Citing famous persons

5.1.5 Use of address forms and speech patterns. In section 5 of the questionnaire on the use of address forms and speech patterns, Japanese respondents were, for the first time, requested to reply to two questions not asked of the American respondents. Both questions deal with the levels of speech, a feature lacking in the American speech community. The first question is: 'When do you use honorifics?' Sixty-five salespeople replied to this question, of whom 34 (52%) said that they use honorifics during the sales contact at all times, regardless of the various personal backgrounds of the customers. The following list shows the age distribution of these 34 salespeople. The percentage is in terms of the total in each age group.

Age: Percent:
Under 20   20.0
21-30   30.5
31-40   44.4
41-50   40.0
51-60   0

Following are the answers of salespeople who use honorifics only under certain circumstances.

Circumstance: No. of respondents:
1. When talking with people of
     a higher social status   17
2. When addressing older people   3
3. When addressing people with whom
     there is no degree of intimacy   1
4. When requesting agreement   1
5. When praising the addressee   1
6. At time of initial encounter   2
7. At beginning and end of the
     encounter   1
8. After the customer's name   2

Only 3 out of 65 (4.6%) answered that they were not conscious of honorifics when engaged in conversational interaction with customers.

Forty-nine salespeople responded to the second question: 'When do you use humble forms?' Of this number, 4 (8.1%) replied that they are not conscious of using humble forms, and 39 (86.6%) replied that they always use humble forms in the course of conversation with the customers, when they are referring to (1) themselves, (2) their company, or (3) someone working for the same company. The age distribution of these 39 salespeople is shown here, with percentages in terms of the total in each age group:

Age: Percent:
Under 20   20.0
21-30   33.3
31-40   50.0
41-50   46.6
51-60   50.0

Three said that they use humble forms when necessary, but did not cite the circumstances in which they feel obliged to use them. Another three answered that they use humble forms when acknowledging admiration and praise offered by their customers. The foregoing analysis of age distribution of salespeople who habitually employ honorific and humble forms shows that the highest percentage of usage falls in the 31 to 40 age bracket, and the next highest percentage in the 41 to 50 category. The high percentage (50%) for the 51 to 60 category for the use of humble forms does not present a reliable conclusion since only two salespersons in this category responded to the questionnaire.

The third and fourth questions in this section are directed again to salespeople in both speech communities. The third question is 'When do you use address forms?' One American salesperson answered: 'It depends on how and why prospect is first contacted, age, position, how long known and relationship established.' His reply implies that there are some conditions in which American salespeople employ address forms with customers. These conditions also relate to the fourth question: 'What kind of address forms do you use?'

Figure 5.1 Use of address forms by salespeople.

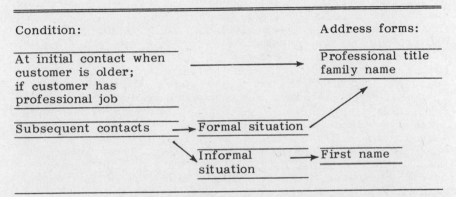

Figure 5.1 illustrates that the use of address forms is conditioned by (1) degree of intimacy, (2) degree of informality, (3) number of contacts with customer, (4) customer's age, and (5) customer's profession. The data from the responses also indicate that the use of address forms varies according to different types of salespeople. For example, two travelling salespeople from publishing companies who are visiting college campuses (informants 1 and 2) said that they always use professional names regardless of the variables (formality, intimacy, time span, customer age, etc.) unless customers specifically ask to be called by first name. Another salesman who visits a doctor's office in the hospital (informant 11) said that he always uses the professional title when he addresses a doctor. A department store salesperson writes: 'The only time the name of a customer is known to me is when he/she presents a charge plate. At that time, when I am returning the plate, I usually address him/her by his/her family name, and again when I complete the sale and give him/her the package.' An insurance salesperson (informant 3) said that he uses the first name if he knows the customer

very well. He also added that if his customers are profession-
als like lawyers, doctors, or university professors, he is careful to use address forms which employ professional title plus
family name. In spite of the varieties in usages on different
occasions and by different types of salespeople, the data tend
to indicate that American salespeople use address forms more
spontaneously than do their Japanese counterparts.

Responses to the same question by Japanese salespeople indicate that they use address forms more consciously and purpose-
fully than the American salespeople. Of 44 Japanese salespeople, 13 replied that they use address forms at the initial
stage of the business transaction. Eight indicated the specific
time when they use address forms as follows: (1) when they want
customers to pay careful attention to their presentation, (2) to
emphasize some specific points in the transaction, (3) when
urging customers to make a decision, and (4) when concluding
their sales contact. Another 12 salespeople simply mentioned
that they use address forms: (1) both at the beginning and the
end, (2) during the conversation and at the end, (3) at pauses
in the conversation, (4) only at the end, and (5) at links between different topics. These answers indicate salespeople's
awareness and effort in the use of address forms for specific
purposes. From these statements, one can conclude that Japanese
salespeople employ address forms as part of a planned technique.
Their use indicates the following functions: (1) to show personal interest in the customer, (2) to make the customer recognize the central point of the transaction, (3) at appropriate
moments in the transaction, (4) to create a good atmosphere
during pauses in the conversation, and (5) to link various
topics in the transaction.

With regard to the next question, 'What kinds of address forms
do you use?', 43 Japanese salespeople answered that they use
professional names and the designations of status in companies,
stores, and hospitals. For example, 6 institutional salespeople
who visit doctors in hospitals replied that they always address
doctors by family name + Sensei, which is an honorific used
for doctors, teachers, politicians, and so forth. Another 27
traveling salespeople who sell electrical appliances, cars,
cosmetics, and school supplies answered that they always address
customers by the status of the companies + San 'an honorific
suffix'. For example, if the salesperson visits a customer who
is president of a certain company, he addresses him as Shachō
San 'president of the company (plus honorific suffix)'. If
the customer is the head of a store, he is called Tenchō San
'head of the store (plus honorific suffix)'. In regard to
general customers, excluding professional people and those in
institutional administrative positions, the data show a variety
of address forms used by the salespeople, and this usage is
related to conditions and mutual relationships between
salespeople and customers. Figure 5.2 lists different kinds of
address forms and conditions for their use.

Figure 5.2 Address forms used by salespeople to ordinary customers in the Japanese speech community.

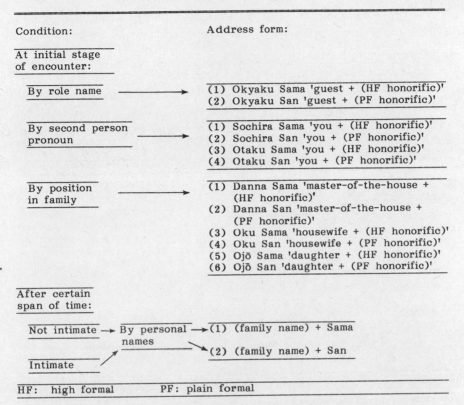

Condition:	Address form:

At initial stage of encounter:

By role name ⟶ (1) Okyaku Sama 'guest + (HF honorific)'
(2) Okyaku San 'guest + (PF honorific)'

By second person pronoun ⟶ (1) Sochira Sama 'you + (HF honorific)'
(2) Sochira San 'you + (PF honorific)'
(3) Otaku Sama 'you + (HF honorific)'
(4) Otaku San 'you + (PF honorific)'

By position in family ⟶ (1) Danna Sama 'master-of-the-house + (HF honorific)'
(2) Danna San 'master-of-the-house + (PF honorific)'
(3) Oku Sama 'housewife + (HF honorific)'
(4) Oku San 'housewife + (PF honorific)'
(5) Ojō Sama 'daughter + (HF honorific)'
(6) Ojō San 'daughter + (PF honorific)'

After certain span of time:

Not intimate ⟶ By personal names ⟶ (1) (family name) + Sama
Intimate ⟶ (2) (family name) + San

HF: high formal   PF: plain formal

As the questionnaire data indicate, these forms of address are the ones commonly used by Japanese salespersons in approaching the ordinary nonprofessional customer or one whose social status is unknown.

In the questionnaire for customers, a similar question appears: 'Do you use address forms when you speak with the salesperson?' Of the American customers, 38.3% answered 'yes', and 33.3% of the Japanese customers responded affirmatively. Those who answered 'yes' were asked to indicate what terms they use in addressing salespeople. Address forms used by American customers are shown in Figure 5.3.

Figure 5.3 shows that address forms become more personalized after prolonged friendly contact with salespeople. At the initial stage, American customers address salespeople by terms signifying respect and male/female designation, or by title plus family name. After more prolonged and familiar contact, customers address salespeople by family name and also by company name.

Figure 5.3 Address forms used by American customers to salespeople.

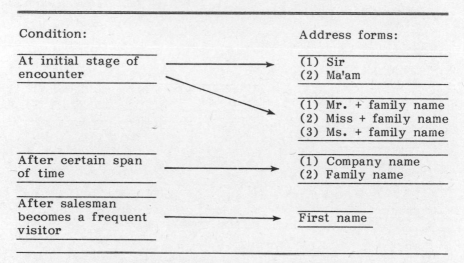

Condition:	Address forms:
At initial stage of encounter	(1) Sir (2) Ma'am
	(1) Mr. + family name (2) Miss + family name (3) Ms. + family name
After certain span of time	(1) Company name (2) Family name
After salesman becomes a frequent visitor	First name

Finally, if the salesperson becomes a frequent visitor, some customers begin to address him/her by first name.

Figure 5.4 Address forms used by Japanese customers to salespeople.

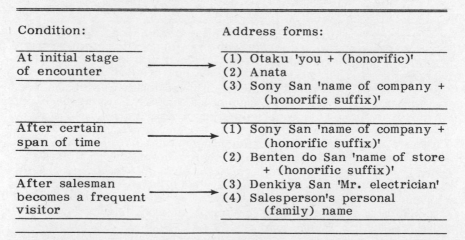

Condition:	Address forms:
At initial stage of encounter	(1) Otaku 'you + (honorific)' (2) Anata (3) Sony San 'name of company + (honorific suffix)'
After certain span of time	(1) Sony San 'name of company + (honorific suffix)' (2) Benten do San 'name of store + (honorific suffix)'
After salesman becomes a frequent visitor	(3) Denkiya San 'Mr. electrician' (4) Salesperson's personal (family) name

Figure 5.4 also indicates different address forms for different occasions. At the initial stage, Japanese salespeople are addressed by customers in terms which signify 'you' in general with honorific suffix. In some cases, if the salesperson's company is famous, he is addressed by the name of his company with honorific suffix. With the passage of time, the sales-

people are addressed by a variety of terms: (1) company name plus honorific suffix; (2) store name plus honorific suffix; (3) name of occupation plus honorific suffix; (4) salesperson's personal name (i.e. usually his/her family name). This variety of address forms does not change even if the salesperson becomes a frequent and sometimes familiar visitor to the customer.

5.1.6 Sales attitudes. The last section in the sales-people's questionnaire concerns sales attitudes: 'Do you consider selling primarily a service or primarily income producing?' The following gives the distribution of answers from American and Japanese salespeople.

Selling is:	A%:	J%:
Service	57.6	25.5
Income producing	18.8	55.3
Service + income producing	14.1	10.1
Not specified	9.4	8.5

Results of asking customers the same question are as follows:

Selling is:	A%:	J%:
Service	32.7	6.4
Income producing	39.5	86.0
Service + income producing	8.1	5.3
Not specified	15.1	2.1

The foregoing results for salespeople and customers indicate the following:

(1) Of the American salespeople, 57.6% consider that selling is primarily a service rather than income producing, while 55.3% of the Japanese salespeople regard selling as primarily income producing rather than as a service.

(2) Only 18.8% of the American salespeople consider that selling is primarily income producing, but 39.5% of the American customers believe that selling is primarily income producing, and this percentage surpasses the percentage of American customers who consider selling primarily a service (32.7%).

(3) Although the percentage is different, both Japanese customers (86%) and Japanese salespeople (55.3%) agree that selling is primarily income producing.

(4) Both American and Japanese customers agree that selling is primarily income producing rather than primarily a service.

The final question for salespeople is: 'What is your image of the ideal salesperson?' The three most frequently cited items from the answers of both speech communities are as follows:

American:	%
1. Knowledgeable	31.7
2. Neat in appearance	20.0
3. Friendly	11.7

Japanese: %
  1. Leaves customers feeling happy   24.4
  2. Is knowledgeable   10.6
  3. Understands and cares for
     customers from customers'
     point of view   7.4

As is indicated, knowledge of the product is indispensable for an ideal salesperson in both speech communities. This is the only quality on which both speech communities agree. The other four qualities are not shared by both speech communities. The second quality cited by American salespeople, neat appearance, agrees with the answers to the question on the qualities of salespersons. There, 68.2% of the American salespeople answered that a salesperson's appearance is very important, but only 29.7% of the Japanese salespeople agreed that it is the most important quality. The third quality pointed out by American salespeople, 'friendly', reaffirms the answers in the section on quality as a salesperson. Under 'friendliness', 78.8% of the American salespeople said that it is very important, while only 42.3% of the Japanese salespeople thought so. The first two items ranked by American salespeople are directly related to the essential function and effort of salespeople. The third item, friendliness, is related to how salespeople behave and talk with customers. However, the first and third items pointed out by Japanese salespeople are closely related with how customers feel after being helped by salespeople. In short, these qualities are evaluated solely from the customers' standpoint rather than from that of the salespeople.

5.2   Analysis of customer questionnaire. The questionnaire for customers has four sections: (1) general information, (2) interaction with salesperson, (3) activities after the speech event, and (4) evaluation and attitude toward salesperson. In the first section, customers are asked to indicate age and sex. In the second section, they are asked (1) how they receive a door-to-door salesperson, (2) how they make contact with the salesperson, (3) their priorities in purchasing the product, (4) how they decline unwanted merchandise, (5) how they take leave, and (6) what kinds of address forms they use and when. Items (3), (5) and (6) of the second section have already been discussed and compared with the responses of salespeople. In the third section, customers are asked if and how they keep in contact with salespeople after the purchase. In the fourth and final section, two questions deal with salesperson's profession and important qualities of salespeople. Both of these have already been discussed and compared with answers obtained from salespeople.

5.2.1   General background. Following is the age and sex distribution of 86 American and 93 Japanese customers.

1. Age:

	American	Japanese
Under 20	1	2
21-30	11	22
31-40	11	52
41-50	12	14
51-60	18	2
Above 60	28	1
Not specified	5	0

2. Sex:

Male	10	10
Female	72	83
Not specified	4	0

5.2.2 Interaction with salesperson. In section (2) of the questionnaire, customers are asked: 'How do you receive a salesperson who comes to visit your home?' Respondents are asked to check one of three answers: (1) ask salesman's name, (2) ask salesman's company, (3) ask both. The results are as follows:

		A%:	J%:
(1)	Ask salesman's name	0	2.1
(2)	Ask salesman's company	23.2	55.9
(3)	Ask both	33.7	9.6

These results indicate that American customers require both names of salesmen and of their companies, while Japanese customers are much more inclined to ask the name of a salesman's company rather than his own name. Of American customers, 19.7% replied that they are not visited by salespeople in their homes, and 16.1% of Japanese customers said that it is always salespeople who begin the conversation by introducing their company. Considering this percentage (16.1) and the percentage of those who said that customers always ask the salesman's company (55.9), it is most likely that, in Japanese society, the company name is considered more important than the salesman's own name, at least during the initial encounter between salesperson and customer.

The next question asks customers to tell how they make contact with a salesperson in a store, according to the following three categories: (1) indicate the reason for visiting the store, (2) simply say that you wish to purchase something, (3) other (specify). A majority of both American and Japanese customers chose the second method, that is, 67.4% of American customers and 91.3% of Japanese customers said that they simply indicate that they want to buy something, rather than giving a more specific reason for visiting the store. When customers decline unwanted merchandise, however, there are differing results from the two speech communities, as follows:

		A%:	J%:
(1)	I don't want this	19.7	12.9
(2)	I'm not interested in the product now	58.1	23.6
(3)	I am undecided now	9.3	9.6
(4)	I will consider it later	9.3	26.8
(5)	I have to ask my husband (wife)	0	7.5
(6)	Other	2.3	19.3
(7)	Not specified	1.1	0

As this list shows, 58.1% of American customers try to decline unwanted merchandise by saying 'I'm not interested in the product now', while 23.6% of Japanese customers use that expression. The list also indicates that 26.8% of Japanese customers (the highest percentage of all the answers given by the Japanese) refuse the purchase by saying, 'I will consider it later'. This is a more indirect refusal, but answers from Japanese customers imply that they sometimes try to refuse in still other ways. Of the Japanese customers who checked the last category, 19.3% mentioned that they usually use the following expressions.

(1) I'm sorry, but I'm satisfied with what I have now.
(2) Please come again, as I'm busy now.
(3) Please forgive me today.

None of these three statements is related to a direct expression of refusal, but the data from the questionnaires show that 18 Japanese customers use this mode of refusal.

5.2.3 Actions after the speech event. Concerning actions with the salesperson after the transaction, customers are asked: 'Do you keep in contact with the salesperson after purchasing the product?' There were 35.4% of the Japanese customers who replied affirmatively, but only 17.4% of the Americans did so. In spite of these different percentages, both American and Japanese customers have similar ways of continuing their contact with salespeople in the following circumstances: (1) when they have problems and questions about the merchandise, (2) when they need further assistance and advice about the product, (3) when some adjustment is necessary, and (4) when the purchase proves defective, etc. The data indicate that there are two ways of continuing contact: (1) by telephone or (2) by returning to the store where the purchase was made. Several customers in both speech communities answered that this sustained relationship is maintained only after major purchases of electrical appliances, furniture, or other expensive items.

CHAPTER SIX

SUMMARY AND CONCLUSION

This study describes and contrasts sales events and salesmen's talk in the American and Japanese speech communities from an ethnographic perspective. Assuming that communication processes in social interaction are culture-specific, the study attempts (1) to investigate overall patterns of sales transactions by taking two particular speech communities as frames of reference, and (2) to identify the social and cultural norms and values which distinguish the sales event in each of these communities. To do this, data were collected and analyzed to discern the verbal behavior of salespeople and customers in their respective roles in a variety of contexts. In addition to the analysis of observed communicative data, both questionnaire and interview techniques were employed to examine the philosophy of buying and selling in the specific social environment in which salespeople and customers interact. These two techniques were used as secondary sources for this investigation and provided valuable background to increase comprehension of the situations.

The findings of the research reaffirm the pragmatic aspect of the theory of human communication, which holds that there is a mutual capacity for understanding between participants in a given speech situation. For example, the data indicate that when a salesperson initiates a transaction, he or she often employs, in the approach stage, various patterns of offer and questions in which form and function are different: e.g. interrogative in form but an offer in function, interrogative in form but a request for information and an offer in function, a statement with an interrogative intonation in form and an offer in function, etc. In this context, the comprehension of different patterns is based on the individual salesperson's knowledge of what to say and how to say it and the hearer's ability to interpret what the salesperson intends to achieve with that particular message.

Other aspects of the study support the view of those who believe that in a social situation people behave in similar fashion regardless of differences in culture, social status, age, personal background, etc. For example, all four examples chosen from both speech communities for the purpose of ethnographic analysis in Chapter 3 demonstrate that turn-taking is a basic functional feature of conversation and that the conversational sequence is composed of chains such as 'abab', where 'a' and 'b' represent participants. Each example cited indicates that during the sales transaction the conversation is carried on by a succession of turns, changing roles between speaker and hearer, between salesperson and customer. Also, in the greeting, approach, pre-closing, and leave-taking stages, the data manifest frequent use of adjacency pairs, which have been cited by ethnomethodologists as a basic structural unit.

Another aspect of the study which seems to support ethnomethodological interest in the process of human interaction is the following: two methods of approach, the 'may-I-serve-you' approach and the 'merchandise' approach, are common to both speech communities. Careful analysis of data indicates that each approach has specific functions, purposes, and characteristics. The study also demonstrates that when the 'merchandise' approach is initiated by customers, salespersons in both speech communities use a 'playback' technique which has two forms: (1) assertive and (2) query. Another feature shared by both speech communities is the use of similar markers to indicate preclosing and leave-taking.

Study of the data of various types of sales events shows certain overall patterns of sales transactions as typical of both speech communities. For regardless of social characteristics of the salespeople (e.g. age, experience, sex, etc.), their different cultural backgrounds, and the different types of sales transactions, the procedures for selling are composed of three principal stages in each of the two speech communities: (1) opening, (2) middle, and (3) closing. Each of these stages consists of standard subcomponents, not all of which are necessarily part of each sales transaction. The first stage includes greeting and identification. The middle stage, the actual business transaction, is usually composed of approach and negotiation. Finally, the closing stage contains pre-closing and leave-taking.

In the first stage, participants exchange greetings and the salesperson identified himself/herself if he or she is not already known to the customer. The middle stage, composed of approach and negotiation, is a transition between the initial exchange of greetings and the actual business transaction. In the approach stage, by employing either the 'may-I-serve-you' approach or the 'merchandise' approach, the salesperson or the customer initiates the transaction. In the negotiation stage, both participants discuss and bargain about the merchandise or service in question. In pre-closing, either the customer or the salesperson or both manifest the desire to terminate the transaction. The transaction ends with leave-taking.

The major part of this study dealt with the ethnographic analysis of the data. Fundamental to the ethnographic point of view is the belief that communication is culture-specific and that each individual speech event is governed by the social and cultural norms, beliefs, and values of a particular speech community. Use of language or ways of speaking can be described in terms of the role relationship between the salesperson and the customer. Since the salesman-customer relationship is a regular pattern of social interaction and each participant has a definite role and status, we can analyze this specific social relationship in terms of rights and obligations of the participants. Thus from an analysis of the data, the responses to the questionnaires, and answers obtained from interviews, it is obvious that sales transactions within the American speech community are typically egalitarian. The basic equality of salesperson and customer can be shown by the following six features.

(1) Both salesperson and customer, regardless of the type of transaction, maintain the same level of informality throughout the conversation.

(2) From the quantitative point of view, the salesperson's and the customer's conversation is usually composed of a more balanced number of moves than its counterpart in the Japanese speech community.

(3) There is no speech pattern of formality and respect except for the use of titles such as *Dr.*, *Mr.*, *Mrs.*, etc.

(4) Greeting formula and conversational formula in pre-closing and leave-taking are all reciprocal.

(5) Address forms are also used interchangeably by both salesperson and customer, and the usage is more flexible according to different situations, e.g. formal and informal situations, time span, degree of intimacy, etc.

(6) The self-identification of the salesperson is carried out mainly on the basis of personal names. This reliance on names stresses contact on a personal level from individual to individual, minimizing status differences.

The fact that a Japanese sales transaction reflects a relationship of relative power between salesperson and customer can be shown by the following ten features.

(1) Regardless of the type of sales transaction, each sales event (except street-hawker and market sales) is characterized by the frequent use of honorifics, polite expressions, and humble forms in a formal style on the part of the salesperson, and by nonuse of honorifics, humble forms, and polite expressions on the part of the customer, who always speaks in an informal style.

(2) Varying degrees of politeness and respect can be expressed on different levels of formality, e.g. low formal, plain formal, and high formal, each of which carries special functions and is composed of different internal structure (e.g. morphological changes in verb ending; addition of honorific prefixes to nouns and verbs; and sentence structure with no agent or

introducing *Kango* in the utterance, etc.). This verbal repertoire of the salesperson is closely related to the following factors: (1) physical distance from the customer, (2) number of customers, and (3) the invisibility of the customers.

(3) The salesperson's formal politeness to the customer is also manifested by the use of specific vocabulary, especially in his manner of refusing a customer's request, and by his desire to carry out the interaction with great formality, deference, and courtesy.

(4) There are abundant conventionalized patterns of greetings, apologies, and expressions of gratitude for salespersons which are more ornate and ritualistic than those used in the American speech community. Each conventional pattern is self-contained and nonreciprocal.

(5) Since Japanese has an established pattern of different lexical items to signify a kinship term used for family members versus those used for outsiders, the salespersons are always careful to use the terms reserved for outsiders which are accompanied by honorific suffixes.

(6) Usage of vocabulary by salespeople is also conventionalized, e.g. *Hitotsu, mata, tokoro,* etc. These stereotyped words are used to emphasize the salesperson's apology and desire to show respect and courtesy.

(7) As protocol for carrying out sales transactions in a more polite and courteous manner, the salesperson uses specific signals (e.g. chiming in with the customer's remark by adding *ha* in a low pitch once or twice, making the formal [ss] noise of respect before asking questions of the customer, and employing a specific word like *yoroshiku*). This ritualistic behavior is usually accompanied by nonverbal facial expressions and gestures, e.g. frequent bows and nodding, etc.

(8) Address terms from the salesperson to the customer are always used with honorific suffixes or titles, and all the address forms are used nonreciprocally.

(9) When salespeople identify themselves, they are inclined to give precedence to the company or institution for which they work. This method stresses awareness of status and occupational role, and lack of self-awareness of the individual in relation to the customer.

(10) Category terms (the name of the salesperson's company or institution and his/her status) used by the customer in addressing the salesperson stress awareness of status and role relationship between customer and addressee, rather than awareness of the communication between two individuals.

These features point up the fact that habitual language choice in sales events is more than merely a matter of an individual's preference; rather it is a function of role relations between salesperson and customer. This relationship is defined by sociocultural norms and expectations in each of the speech communities considered.

Although the speech pattern of sales events in the Japanese speech community is characterized by the relative power relationship in the sense that it is always the salesperson who should show respect for the customer, the data indicate that in specific instances when the salesperson and the customer have the same status, the role relationship between two participants becomes ambiguous and hence their speech patterns also deviate from the usual salesperson-customer pattern. The data also manifest that this deviation in the speech pattern of the salesperson is due to deliberate violation of discourse rules by street-hawkers and market salespeople. In these two specific types of transactions, the relative power in the relationship between street-hawkers and market salespeople and their customers is reversed and it is the salespeople who appear to dominate in the power relationship. For their speech does not utilize honorifics, polite expressions, and formal styles, but instead includes such features as commands.

According to Bernstein (1964), linguistic interaction can be most fruitfully examined by observing and analyzing how participants in the discourse achieve decision-making. In my study, I suggest that recognition of the principles of negotiation procedures in sales events facilitates understanding of the ways of speaking in each speech community. Analysis of the data and information obtained from questionnaires and interviews all demonstrate that salespeople as well as customers in the American speech community tend to exchange their opinions more personally and more directly by offering personal comment freely and forthrightly. On the other hand, one can observe that both salespersons and customers in the Japanese speech community are more concerned with using appropriate standard forms in the appropriate contexts and render their desired image more indirectly.

In sales events another cultural difference between the Japanese and American speech communities becomes apparent when one considers the salesperson's verbal behavior toward the customer in a face-to-face situation. Although he or she is, of course, interested in the outcome of the sale, the typical American salesperson never subordinates his or her personal individuality to his or her role as a salesperson. In the Japanese speech community, however, roles and expectations are much more pronounced. Consequently, Japanese salespeople suspend their individuality in order to fulfill their occupational role and to meet fully the expectations imposed by their society. These findings seem to correlate with the concept of personal and transactional interactions discussed by Gumperz (1964).

The difference between the American and Japanese speech communities described in detail throughout this study and summarized here must be rooted in underlying norms and beliefs peculiar to each of the two speech communities. The final section of this study is devoted to identifying these norms which produce different ways of speaking unique to each society.

I offer these findings as one who is a member of the Japanese speech community and a very interested observer of the American speech community. My discussion of social and cultural norms is therefore directed principally to the analysis of my own speech community, with which I am, naturally, more familiar.

As a Japanese, I often feel ill at ease (or at least not perfectly comfortable) during a social encounter with another Japanese, when I do not have a clear picture of the other person's social background. In other words, if I cannot identify the other person's status vis-à-vis myself, it is hard for me to establish a proper relationship with him or her, at least in our initial face-to-face encounter. This personal attitude is further explained in a statement about my native culture by a Japanese anthropologist.

> In everyday affairs, a man who has no awareness of relative rank is not able to speak or even sit and eat. When speaking, he is expected always to be ready with differentiated, delicate degree of honorific expressions appropriate to the rank order between himself and the person he addresses (Nakane 1970:31).

Nakane's statement points up the fact that in the Japanese speech community, the one to whom one is speaking is the essential factor in determining *how* one speaks. Nakane continues thus:

> Without consciousness of ranking, life could not be carried on smoothly in Japan, for rank is the social norm on which Japanese life is based (p. 33).

This pivotal concept of awareness of rank, deeply rooted in Japanese social behavior, has also been noted by the Western anthropologist, Benedict (1946:43).

> Japan's confidence in hierarchy is basic in her whole notion of man's relation to his fellow man and man's relation to the state.

Commenting on how Japanese people define rank, Nakane explains that status is a dominant factor. My entire study strongly supports Nakane's hypothesis that the Japanese stress situational position in a particular frame, rather than universal attribute, when they identify professional status and role. For example, my analyses of data, questionnaires, and interviews indicate that when Japanese salespeople identify themselves and when Japanese customers identify Japanese salespeople, both salespeople and customers are inclined to give precedence to company or institution over the salespeople's personal attributes by identifying or asking the names of the salespeople's companies rather than identifying or asking their personal names.

Another characteristic of this necessity to rank in Japanese society is that once the specific relationships of the Japanese interpersonal pairs are defined according to status and role of each member (e.g. student-teacher, employer-employee, senior-junior, etc.), the participants are required to play their fixed roles in all places where they meet, even if they are different. Thus,

A superior in one's place of work is always one's superior wherever he is met, at a restaurant, at home, in the street (Nakane, p. 34).

Furthermore, these fixed roles of interpersonal pairs are virtually immune to changes in time. The following statement by a Japanese sociolinguist attests to this view. His explicit comparison between the two distinct sociocultural norms underlying the American and Japanese speech communities is especially interesting.

When American graduate students earn their doctorates, they soon start calling their former professors by their first names. The reason is that in the U.S. the concept of colleagueship is an egalitarian one and supersedes differences in seniority, scholarship or age. In contrast, I still cannot call an old professor from my university days by any term other than *Sensei* 'teacher'. This is more than twenty years after graduation (Suzuki 1978:140-141).

Another social and cultural norm which is unique to Japanese society is the mode of verbal interaction in the communication procedure. According to Suzuki,

It is frequently pointed out that whereas Western culture is based on the distinction between the observer and the observed, on the opposition of the self versus the other, Japanese culture and sentiment show a strong tendency to overcome this distinction by having the self immerse itself in the other (1978:145).

Suzuki's statement regarding assimilating oneself with the other in Japanese culture can be illustrated by the following example.

When a Japanese communicates with another Japanese, the speaker in the conversation feels more comfortable waiting to ascertain the addressee's feelings and thoughts than actively expressing his or her own opinions. This is a general phenomenon that goes beyond the role relationship between sales people and customers documented in this study. Faculty meetings in the Japanese college where I used to teach clearly illustrate this cultural phenomenon. In Japan, the professor who expresses his own opinions usually uses circumlocutions and maintains a rather strict reserve in order not to hurt professors who hold opposing views. Even if he has been invited to contribute his opinion, he behaves in the same manner. When a Japanese professor wants to agree with his fellow professors, he expresses his intention of agreement with an abundance of rhetorical expressions. When he really wants to disagree, he begins his speech by citing some good points in the opinions with which he cannot totally agree, but he never directly expresses his intention to disagree.

Attending faculty meetings in the United States was for me a totally different experience. American professors seem to enjoy exchanging different views frankly and forthrightly, and do not try to avoid direct verbal confrontations with regard to conflicting views. Here, the speaker confronts the addressee and expresses his opinion directly. Terasawa (1974) explained this difference in communication procedures between these two cultures by employing the terms 'you-to-you' approach and 'I-to-you' approach, referring to the Japanese versus the American speech community.

Analyses of data, questionnaires, and interviews in this study reveal in sales transactions a phenomenon similar to that described here in regard to faculty meetings. In the negotiation stage, the vast majority of Japanese salespersons try to convince their customers to buy by inviting the purchase indirectly and politely. Likewise, Japanese customers have a tendency to refuse unwanted merchandise circuitously rather than directly. This underlying norm of other-oriented, indirect communication helps to explain why we Japanese often refer to our own culture as sasshi no bunka 'guessing culture'.

The study reaffirms a basic assumption of sociolinguistics that verbal behavior can only be understood in terms of the social dimensions of language. By observing language choice and use within a social situation, the study demonstrates that language cannot be effectively investigated in isolation from its social setting.

It is my hope that research and analysis such as this will help to promote intercultural understanding and facilitate communication not only in this very practical area but in all the other areas and aspects of our lives.

APPENDIX 1

QUESTIONS FOR INTERVIEWEES

1. General information
    1.1 What kind of salesperson are you?
    1.2 What types of merchandise or services do you handle?
    1.3 How many years of experience have you as a salesperson?
    1.4 How old are you and what is your educational background?

2. Basic principles of salespersonship
    2.1 Do you pay special attention to your appearance?
    2.2 Do you think it important to study the product you represent? Why?
    2.3 How do you identify yourself to your prospective customers?

3. Professional qualities as a salesperson
    3.1 What do you think of the following qualities as salesperson?: appearance, manner, speech pattern, persuasiveness, friendliness, tolerance, kindness, consistency in personality, enthusiasm, ability to discern customer's response, honesty and sincerity.
    3.2 What do you think of the following skills as salesperson?: key words, good grammar, logical presentation, fluency, pronunciation, facial expression, tone of voice, eye contact, gestures and body posture.

4. Sales technique and strategies
    4.1 Do you make specific preparation for a sales contact besides study of your product? How?
    4.2 How do you initiate your conversation with your customer?
    4.3 How do you negotiate with your customers? For example, how do you reply to customers' objections, preferences for other brands, etc.?
    4.4 When you succeed in selling your merchandise, what do you do?

4.5 When you do not succeed in selling your merchandise, what do you do?

4.6 How do you take leave of the customer: (1) after a successful sale? (2) after no sale?

4.7 How do you discern whether or not he or she is a prospective customer?

5. Use of address forms and speech patterns
   5.1 When do you use address forms? What kinds?
   5.2 When do you use honorifics? (Japanese salespeople only)
   5.3 When do you use humble forms? (Japanese salespeople only)

6. Sales attitudes
   6.1 Do you consider selling primarily a service or primarily income producing?
   6.2 What is your image of the ideal salesperson?

APPENDIX 2

QUESTIONNAIRE FOR SALESPERSONS

1. General information.   Please check or fill in appropriate category.
   1.1 Age: (1) 20 or under ... (2) 21-30 ... (3) 31-40 ...
        (4) 41-50 ... (5) 51-60 ... (6) Over 60 ...
   1.2 Sex: (1) Male ... (2) Female ...
   1.3 Type of salesperson, e.g. traveling, direct, store, etc. (specify) ...
   1.4 Types of merchandise and services: (1) Medicine ...
        (2) Cosmetics ... (3) Insurance ... (4) Automobiles ... (5) Other (specify) ...
   1.5 Years of experience: ...
   1.6 Educational background: (1) College ... (2) High school ... (3) Other (specify) ...

2. Examination of salespersonship
   2.1 To what degree do you pay special attention to your appearance? 'Great deal' vs. 'not at all' on a five-point scale ...
   2.2 To what degree do you think it important to study the product you represent? 'Great deal' vs. 'not at all' on a five-point scale ...
   2.3 How do you identify yourself to your prospective customers? (1) By first indicating your name and then the name of your company ... (2) By first indicating the name of your company and then your name ... (3) By first indicating the name of your company and then your name with your business card ... (4) Other (specify) ...
   2.4 What are your priorities among these variables when you explain your product to the customer?   Place (1) beside the most important, (2) next in importance, etc.: Cost ... Quality ... Convenience ... Appearance ... Practicality ... Beauty ... Other (specify) ...

151

3. Qualities and skills as salesperson
   3.1 On a five-point scale, to what degree do you consider the following qualities as a salesperson 'very important' vs. 'not important at all'? Appearance ... Manner ... Speech pattern ... Persuasiveness ... Friendliness ... Tolerance ... Kindness ... Consistency in personality ... Enthusiasm ... Ability to discern customer's response ... Honesty and sincerity ...
   3.2 On a five-point scale, to what degree do you consider the following skills as a salesperson 'very important' vs. 'not important at all'? Key words ... Good grammar ... Logical presentation ... Fluency ... Pronunciation ... Facial expression ... Tone of voice ... Eye contact ... Gestures ... Body posture ...

4. Sales technique
   4.1 Do you make specific preparation for a sales contact besides study of your product and personal appearance? Yes ... No ... If yes, please explain.
   4.2 How do you initiate conversation with your customer? Please explain ...
   4.3 How do you negotiate, that is, how do you reply to customers' objections, preferences for other brands, etc.? ...
   4.4 When you succeed in selling your merchandise, what do you do? ...
   4.5 When you do not succeed in selling your merchandise, what do you do? ...
   4.6 How do you take leave of the customer: (1) after a successful sale? ... (2) after no sale? ...
   4.7 How do you discern whether or not he or she is a prospective customer? ...
   4.8 How do you convince the customer to buy? What are your priorities among these variables? Place (1) beside the most important, (2) next in importance, etc.: By demonstration ... By explaining the advantages of the product ... By presenting statistical results ... By citing use of product by famous persons ... By comparing with competitive products or services ... Other (specify) ...

5. Use of address forms and speech patterns
   5.1 When do you use address forms?
   5.2 What kinds of address forms do you use, e.g. customer's family name, first name, position, etc.?
   5.3 When do you use honorifics? (Japanese salespeople only)
   5.4 When do you use humble forms? (Japanese salespeople only)

6. Sales attitudes
    6.1 Do you consider selling primarily a service or primarily income producing?
    6.2 What is your image of the ideal salesperson?

APPENDIX 3

QUESTIONNAIRE FOR CUSTOMERS

1. General information. Please check appropriate category.
   1.1 Age: (1) 20 or under ... (2) 21-30 ... (3) 31-40 ...
       (4) 41-50 ... (5) 51-60 ... (6) Over 60 ...
   1.2 Sex: (1) Male ... (2) Female ...

2. Interaction with salesperson
   2.1 How do you receive a salesperson who comes to visit
       your home? (1) Ask salesperson's name ... (2) Ask
       salesperson's company ... (3) Ask both ... (4) Other
       (specify) ...
   2.2 How do you make contact with the salesperson in the
       store? (1) Indicate the reason for visiting the
       store ... (2) Simply say that you wish to purchase
       something ...
   2.3 What are your priorities among these variables in pur-
       chasing the product? Place (1) beside the most
       important, (2) next in importance, etc.: Cost ...
       Quality ... Convenience ... Appearance ... Practical-
       ity ... Beauty ... Other (specify) ...
   2.4 How do you decline to purchase unwanted merchandise?
       Directly ... Indirectly ... Check the appropriate ex-
       pression: I don't want this ... I am not interested
       in the produce now ... I am undecided now ... I will
       consider it later ... I have to ask my husband (wife)
       ... Other (specify) ...
   2.5 How do you take leave: (1) after you buy? ... (2)
       after no sale? ...
   2.6 Do you use address forms when you speak with the sales-
       person? Yes ... No ... If yes, what kinds of terms
       do you use, e.g. salesperson's family name, sales-
       person's company name, salesperson's first name,
       etc.?

3. Activities after the speech event
   3.1 Do you keep in contact with the salesperson after pur-
       chasing a product? Yes ... No ... If yes, how?

4. Evaluation of and attitudes toward salesperson
    4.1 Do you think that the salesperson's profession is a service or simply an occupation? Why?
    4.2 On a five-point scale, to what degree do you consider the following qualities as a salesperson 'very important' vs. 'not important at all'? Appearance ... Manner ... Speech pattern ... Persuasiveness ... Friendliness ... Tolerance ... Kindness ... Consistency in personality ... Enthusiasm ... Ability to discern customer's response ... Honesty and sincerity ...

BIBLIOGRAPHY

Austin, J. L. 1962. How to do things with words. Oxford: Clarendon Press.

Basso, K. H. 1972. To give up on words. In: Language and social context. Edited by Pier A. Giglioli. Middlesex, England: Penguin Education. 67-86.

Bauman, R., and J. Sherzer, eds. The ethnography of speaking. In: Annual Review of Anthropology. Stanford, Calif.: Stanford University.

Bellack, A. A., H. M. Kliebard, R. T. Hyman, and F. L. Smith. 1966. The language of the classroom. New York: Teachers College Press.

Benedict, Ruth. 1946. The chrysanthemum and the sword. Cambridge, Mass.: Houghton Mifflin.

Bernstein, Basil. 1964. Elaborated and restricted codes: Their social origins and some consequences. American Anthropologist 66.6, Part 2:55-69.

Birdwhistell, Ray L. 1970. Kinesics and context: Essays on body motion communication. Philadelphia: University of Pennsylvania Press.

Blom, Jan-Petter, and John J. Gumperz. 1972. Social meaning in linguistic structure: Code-switching in Norway. In: Gumperz and Hymes, eds. (1972:407-434).

Bloomfield, Leonard. 1933. Language. New York: Henry Holt.

Brown, Roger, and Albert Gilman. 1968. The pronouns of power and solidarity. In: Readings in the sociology of language. Edited by Joshua A. Fishman. The Hague: Mouton. 252-275.

Burling, Robbins. 1969. Linguistics and ethnographic description. American Anthropologist 71:817-827.

Chomsky, Noam. 1957. Syntactic structures. The Hague: Mouton.

Chomsky, Noam. 1965. Aspects of the theory of syntax. Cambridge, Mass.: MIT Press.

Chomsky, Noam. 1968. Language and mind. (Enlarged edition, 1972.) New York: Harcourt Brace.

Coulthard, Malcolm. 1977. An introduction to discourse analysis. London: Longman.

157

Duncan, S.D. 1972. Some signals and rules for taking turns in conversation. Journal of Personality and Social Psychology 23.283-292.

Duncan, S. D. 1973. Towards a grammar for dyadic conversation. Semiotica 9.1:29-46.

Duncan, S. D. 1974. On the structure of speaker-auditor interaction during speaking turns. Language in Society 3.2:161-180.

Dundes, Alan. 1962. From etic to emic units in the structural study of folktales. Journal of American Folklore 75.95-105.

Elzinga, R. H. 1975. Nonverbal communication: Body accessibility among Japanese. Psychologia 18.205-211.

Ervin-Tripp, Susan. 1973. Language acquisition and communicative choice. Stanford, Calif.: Stanford University Press.

Ferguson, Charles A. 1959. Diglossia. Word 15.325-340.

Firth, J. R. 1935. The technique of semantics. In: Papers in Linguistics 1934-1951. London: Oxford University Press, 1957. 7-33.

Fischer, J. L. 1964. Words for self and others in some Japanese families. American Anthropologist 66.6, Part 2:115-126.

Frake, Charles O. 1964. Notes on queries in ethnography. In: Cognitive anthropology. Edited by Stephen A. Tyler. New York: Holt, Rinehart and Winston. 123-136.

Fraser, Bruce. 1974. An analysis of vernacular performative verb. In: Toward tomorrow's linguistics. Edited by Roger W. Shuy and Charles-James N. Bailey. Washington, D.C.: Georgetown University Press. 139-158.

Garfinkel, H. 1967. Studies in ethnomethodology. Englewood Cliffs: Prentice-Hall.

Girard, Joe. 1977. How to sell anything to anybody. New York: Warner Books.

Goffman, Erving. 1959. The presentation of self in everyday life. New York: Doubleday.

Goffman, Erving. 1963. Behavior in public places. Glencoe, N.Y.: Free Press.

Goffman, Erving. 1967a. Strategic interaction. New York: Ballantine Books.

Goffman, Erving. 1967b. Interaction ritual: Essays on face-to-face behavior. New York: Doubleday.

Goffman, Erving. 1971. Relations in public: Micro studies of the public order. New York: Basic Books.

Goffman, Erving. 1972. The neglected situation. In: Language and social context. Edited by Peter P. Giglioli. Middlesex, England: Penguin Education. 61-66.

Goldstein, Bernice Z., and Kyoko Tamura. n.d. Japan and America: A comparative study in language and culture. Tokyo: Charles Tuttle.

Gordon, D., and G. Lakoff. 1971. Conversational postulates. In: Papers from the Seventh Regional Meeting. Edited by D. Adams, M. A. Campbell, V. Cohen, et al. Chicago: Chicago Linguistic Society. 63-84.

Grice, H. P. 1975. Logic and conversation. In: Syntax and semantics: Speech acts. Edited by Peter Cole and Jerry Morgan. New York: Academic Press. 41-58.

Gumperz, John. 1964. Linguistic and social interaction in two communities. American Anthropologist 66.6, Part 2:137-154.

Gumperz, John J. 1976. Language, communication and public negotiation. In: Anthropology and the public interest: Fieldwork and theory. Edited by P. Sanday. New York: Academic Press. 273-292.

Gumperz, John J. 1977. Sociocultural knowledge in conversational inference. In: Georgetown University Round Table on Languages and Linguistics 1977. Edited by Muriel Saville-Troike. Washington, D.C.: Georgetown University Press. 191-211.

Gumperz, John J., and Dell Hymes, eds. 1972. Directions in sociolinguistics: The ethnography of communication. New York: Holt, Rinehart and Winston.

Hinds, John V. 1976. Aspects of Japanese discourse structure. Tokyo: Kaitakusha.

Hymes, Dell. 1962. The ethnography of speaking. In: Anthropology and human behavior. Edited by T. Gladwin and W. C. Sturtevant. Washington, D.C.: Anthropological Society of Washington. 13-53.

Hymes, Dell. 1964a. Introduction: Toward ethnographies of communication. American Anthropologist 66.6, Part 2:1-34.

Hymes, Dell, ed. 1964b. Language in culture and society. New York: Harper and Row.

Hymes, Dell. 1964c. A perspective for linguistic anthropology. In: Horizons of anthropology. Edited by Sol Tax. London: Aldine. 92-107.

Hymes, Dell. 1967a. Models of the interaction of language and social setting. Journal of Social Issues. 23.2:8-28.

Hymes, Dell. 1967b. The anthropology of communication. In: Human communication. Edited by F. E. X. Dance. New York: Holt, Rinehart and Winston. 1-39.

Hymes, Dell. 1971. Sociolinguistics and the ethnography of speaking. In: Social anthropology and language. Edited by Edwin Ardener. New York: Tavistock. 47-93.

Hymes, Dell. 1972. Models of the interaction of language and social life. In: Gumperz and Hymes, eds. (1972:35-71).

Hymes, Dell. 1973. Toward ethnographies of communication. In: Intercommunication among nations and peoples. Edited by Michael H. Prosser. New York: Harper and Row. 45-66.

Hymes, Dell. 1974. Foundations in sociolinguistics: An ethnographic approach. Philadelphia: University of Pennsylvania Press.

Irvine, Judith T. 1974. Strategies of status manipulation in the Wolof-greeting. In: Exploration in the ethnography of speaking. Edited by Richard Bauman and Joel Sherzer. London: Cambridge University Press. 167-191.

Jakobson, R. 1972. Nonverbal signs for 'yes' and 'no.' Language in Society 1.1:91-96.

Jefferson, Gail. 1972. Side sequence. In: Sudnow, ed. (1972: 294-338).

Karttunen, Lauri. 1977. Presupposition and linguistic context. In: Proceedings of the Texas Conference on Performatives, Presuppositions, and Implicatures. Edited by Andy Rogers, Bob Wall, and John P. Murphy. Washington, D.C.: Center for Applied Linguistics. 149-160.

Keenan, Edward L. 1971. Two kinds of presupposition in natural language. In: Studies in linguistic semantics. Edited by C. J. Fillmore and D. T. Langendoen. New York: Holt, Rinehart and Winston. 42-60.

Keenan, Elinor O. 1976. The universality of conversational postulates. Language in Society 5.67-80.

Kendon, A. 1967. Some functions of gaze direction in social interaction. Acta Psychologica 26.22-63.

Kokuritsu Kokugo Kenkyū Sho (The National Language Research Institute). 1951. Gendai go no joshi, jodōshi: Yōhō to jitsurei (Particles and auxiliary verbs in modern Japanese: Usages and examples). Tokyo: Shūei Shuppan.

Kokuritsu Kokugo Kenkyū Sho. 1957. Keigo to keigo ishiki (Honorifics and awareness of honorifics). Tokyo: Shūei Shuppan.

Kuno, Susumu. 1978. Danwa no bunpo (Grammar of discourse). Tokyo: Taishūkan.

Kurokawa, Shōzo. 1972. Japanese terms of address: Some usages of the first and second person pronouns. Papers in Japanese Linguistics 1, Part 2:228-236.

Labov, William. 1966. The social stratification of English in New York City. Washington, D.C.: Center for Applied Linguistics.

Labov, William. 1970 The study of language in its social context. Studium Generale 23.30-87.

Labov, William. 1972. Rule for ritual insults. In: Sudnow, ed. (1972:120-169).

Labov, William. 1977. Therapeutic discourse. New York: Academic Press.

Lakoff, Robin. 1971. If's, and's and but's about conjunction. In: Studies in linguistic semantics. Edited by C. J. Fillmore and D. T. Langendoen. New York: Holt, Rinehart and Winston. 115-149.

Lakoff, Robin. 1972. Language in context. Lg. 48.4:907-927.

Lyons, J. 1968. Introduction to theoretical linguistics. Cambridge: Cambridge University Press.

Lyons, J. 1970a. Chomsky. London: Fontana/William Collins.

Lyons, J., ed. 1970b. New horizons in linguistics. Harmondsworth, England: Penguin.

Merritt, Marilyn. 1977. The playback: An instance of variation in discourse. In: Studies in language variation.

Edited by Ralph W. Fasold and Roger W. Shuy. Washington, D.C.: Georgetown University Press. 198-208.

Metzger, Duane, and Gerald E. Williams. 1963. A formal ethnographic analysis of Tenejapa Ladino weddings. American Anthropologist 65.1076-1101.

Miller, Roy A. 1967. The Japanese language. Chicago: University of Chicago Press.

Mitchell, T. F. 1957. The language of buying and selling in Cyrenaica: A situational statement. Hesperis 44.31-71.

Miyaji, Yutaka. 1971. Gendai no keigo (Honorifics of today). In: Kokugoshi 5 (History of the Japanese language): Keigoshi (History of honorifics). Edited by Toshiki Tsujimura. Tokyo: Shūeisha. 367-423.

Moroboshi, Ryū. 1960. Sales no wajutsu to engi (Sales technique). Tokyo: Shunju Sha.

Murayama, Takehisa. 1977. Salesmen no sodate kata (How to train salesmen). Tokyo: Toyo Keizai Shinho Sha.

Nakane, Chie. 1970. Japanese society. Middlesex, England: Penguin.

O'Brien, Gary. 1980. 127 sales closes that work: How to get that 'yes' response in any sales situation. New York: Hawthorn.

Okada, Barbara, and Nancy Taeko Okada. 1973. Do's and don'ts for the Japanese businessman abroad. New York: Regents.

Okushiro, Yoshiharu. 1973. Kyōgō sales no himitsu (Secret of sales). Tokyo: Jitsugyō no Nippon Sha.

Parten, Mildred. 1950. Surveys, polls, and samples: Practical procedures. New York: Harper.

Pike, K. L. 1967. Language in relation to a unified theory of the structure of human behavior. The Hague: Mouton.

Reishauer, Edwin O. 1977. The Japanese. Cambridge, Mass.: Belknap Press of Harvard University Press.

Ross, J. R. 1970. On declarative sentences. In: Readings in English transformational grammar. Edited by R. A. Jacobs and P. S. Rosenbaum. Washington, D.C.: Georgetown University Press. 222-272.

Sacks, H. 1972a. An initial investigation of the usability of conversational data for doing sociology. In: Sudnow, ed. (1972:31-74).

Sacks, H. 1972b. On the analyzability of stories by children. In: Gumperz and Hymes, eds. (1972:325-345).

Sacks, H., E. Schegloff, and G. Jefferson. 1974. A simplest systematics for the organization of turn-taking for conversation. Lg. 50.4:696-735.

Sadock, Jerrold M. 1974. Toward a linguistic theory of speech acts. New York: Academic Press.

Sakagawa, Sakio. 1977. Ureru wajutsu wa doko ga chigau ka (Words that make people buy). Tokyo: Keirin Shobō.

Sakajō, Hajime. 1977. Sales ni seiko suru hanashi kata (Talking your way to success). Tokyo: Keirin Shobō.

Salmond, Anne. 1974. Rituals of encounter among the Maori: Sociolinguistic study of a scene. In: Explorations in the ethnography of speaking. Edited by Richard Bauman and Joel Sherzer. London: Cambridge University Press. 192-212.

Sanches, Mary, and Ben G. Blount, eds. 1975. Sociocultural dimensions of language use: Advances in the study of cognition. New York: Academic Press.

Saussure, Ferdinand. 1915. Cours de linguistique générale. English edition, Course in general linguistics. Edited by Charles Bally and Albert Secheaye. Translated by Wade Baskin. New York: McGraw-Hill, 1966.

Schegloff, Emmanuel A. 1972a. Sequencing in conversational openings. In: Gumperz and Hymes, eds. (1972:346-380).

Schegloff, Emmanuel A. 1972b. Notes on a conversational practice: Formulating place. In: Sudnow, ed. (1972:75-119).

Schegloff, Emmanuel A., and H. Sacks. 1973. Opening up closings. Semiotica 8.4:289-327.

Schenkein, Jim, ed. 1978. Studies in the organizations of conversational interaction. New York: Academic Press.

Searle, J. 1969. Speech acts. New York and London: Cambridge University Press.

Searle, J. 1972. What is a speech act? In: Language and social context. Edited by Pier P. Giglioli. Middlesex, England: Penguin Education. 136-156.

Searle, J. 1975. Indirect speech act. In: Syntax and semantics, Vol. 3: Speech acts. Edited by P. Cole and J. L. Morgan. New York: Academic Press. 59-82.

Seward, Jack. 1968. Japanese in action. New York: Weatherhill.

Seward, Jack. 1972. The Japanese. New York: William Morrow.

Sherzer, Joel. 1974. Namakke, sunmakke, kormakke: Three types of Cuna speech event. In: Explorations in the ethnography of speaking. Edited by R. Bauman and J. Sherzer. London: Cambridge University Press. 262-282.

Sherzer, Joel. 1977. The ethnography of speaking: A critical appraisal. In: Georgetown University Round Table 1977. Edited by Muriel Saville-Troike. Washington, D.C.: Georgetown University Press. 43-57.

Shinpo, Tamihachi. 1979. Ureru kotoba kawaseru kotoba (Words for selling and promoting sales). Tokyo: Dōbunkan.

Sinclair, J. McH., and R. M. Coulthard. 1975. Towards an analysis of discourse: The English used by teachers and pupils. London: Oxford University Press.

Slobin, Dan I. 1967. A field manual for cross-cultural study of the acquisition of communicative competence. Berkeley: University of California.

Smith, A. G., ed. 1960. Communication and culture: Readings in the codes of human interaction. New York: Holt, Rinehart and Winston.

Stalnaker, Robert C. 1977. Pragmatic presuppositions. In: Proceedings of the Texas Conference on Performatives, Presuppositions, and Implicatures. Edited by Andy Rogers, Bob Wall, and John P. Murphy. Washington, D.C.: Center for Applied Linguistics. 135-147.

Sudnow, David, ed. 1972. Studies in social interaction. New York: Free Press.

Suzuki, Takao. 1972. Nihongo no jishōshi (Terms for self-reference in Japanese). In: Nihon bunka to sekai (Japanese culture and the world). Edited by Takao Umesao and Michitaro Tada. Tokyo: Kōdansha. 216-225.

Suzuki, Takao. 1978. Japanese and the Japanese: Words in culture. Translated by Akira Miura. Tokyo: Kōdansha International.

Terasawa, Yoshio. 1974. Japanese style in decision-making. The New York Times, May 12.

Tsuda, Aoi. 1973. Language and mind: A study of Chomsky's theory. Unpublished M.A. thesis. Sophia University, Tokyo.

Tsuda, Aoi. 1974. A critique of I.C. analysis. In: Kiyō: Studies in English literature. Okayama: Notre Dame Seishin University. 63-76.

Tsuda Aoi. 1975. Concept of form: Analysis of three theorists. In: Kiyō: Studies in English literature. Okayama: Notre Dame Seishin University. 53-80.

Tsuda, Aoi. 1978. An ethnographic analysis of American and Japanese speech communities. Unpublished MS.

Warren, Roland L. 1965. Studying your community. New York: Free Press.

Wheeler, Elmer. 1937. Tested sentences that sell. New York: Prentice-Hall.

Wheeler, Elmer. 1941. Tested retail selling. New York: Prentice-Hall.

Wheeler, Elmer. 1957. Tested ways to close the sale. New York: Harper.

Wolfram, Walter A., and Ralph W. Fasold. 1974. The study of social dialects in American English. Englewood Cliffs, N.J.: Prentice-Hall.

Wolfson, Nessa. 1976. Speech events and natural speech: Some implications for sociolinguistic methodology. Language in Society 5.189-209.

Young, Pauline V. 1956. Scientific social surveys and research: An introduction to the background, context, methods, principles and analysis of social studies. Englewood Cliffs, N.J.: Prentice-Hall.